To Joe,

Harvey Pekar

THE Quitter

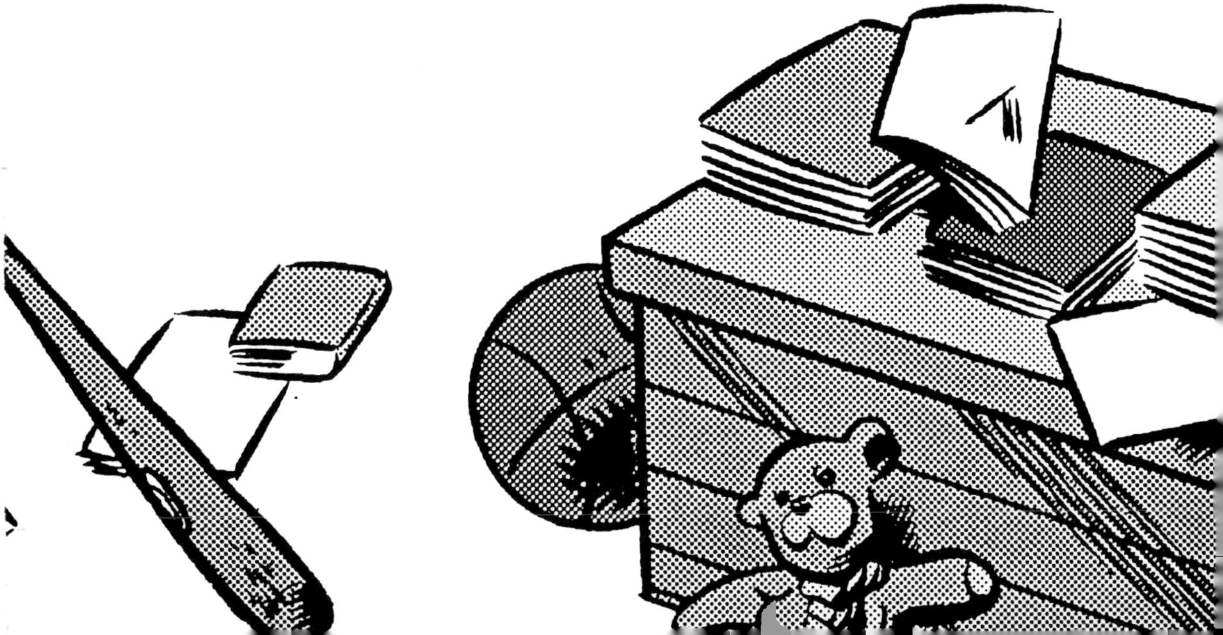

THE Quitter

HARVEY PEKAR Writer **DEAN HASPIEL** Artist **LEE LOUGHRIDGE** Gray Tones **PAT BROSSEAU** Letters

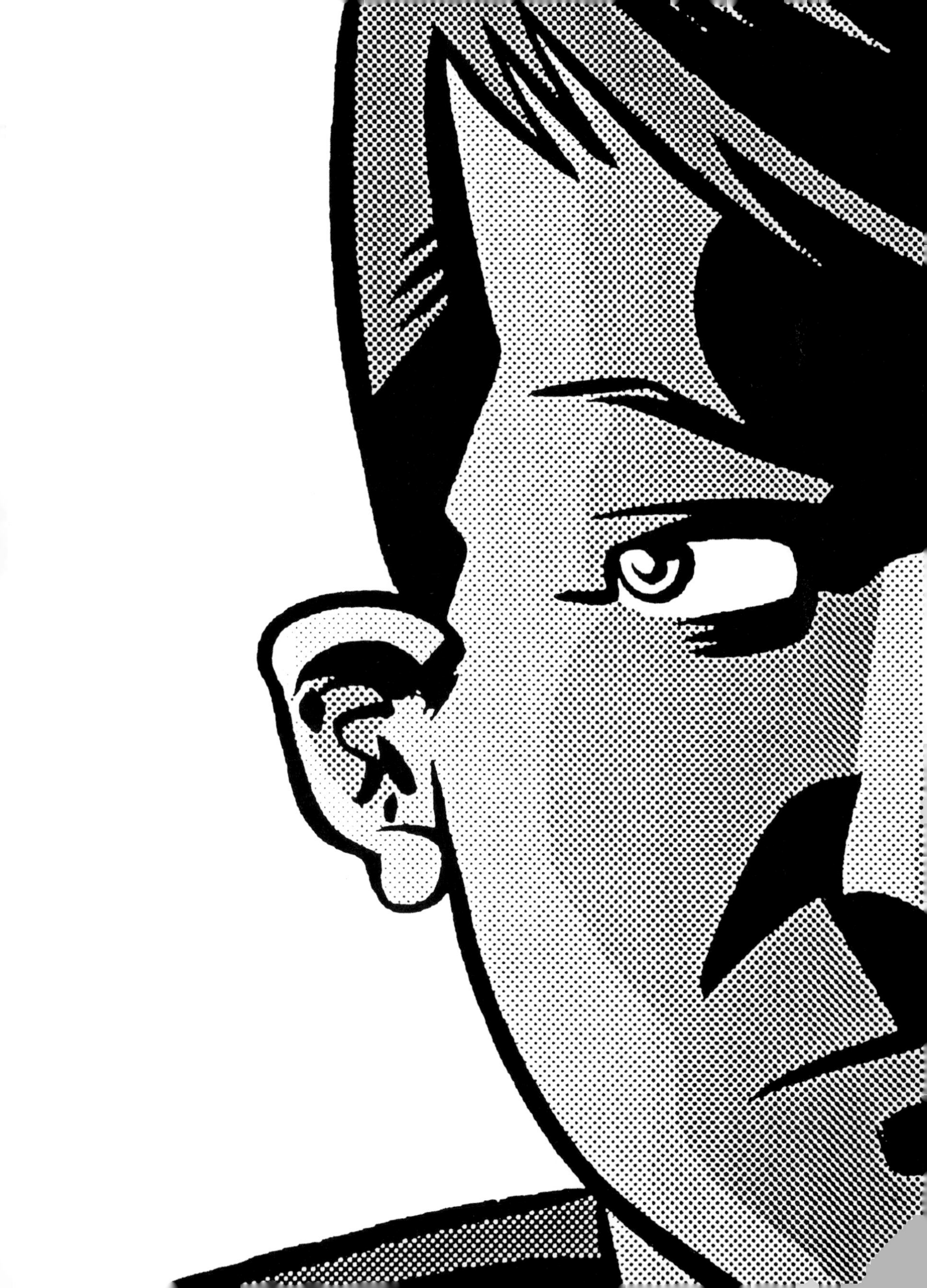

Karen Berger, VP-Executive Editor **Jonathan Vankin**, Editor **Louis Prandi**, Art Director **Paul Levitz**, President & Publisher
Georg Brewer, VP-Design & Retail Product Development **Richard Bruning**, Sr.VP-Creative Director **Patrick Caldon**, Sr.VP-Finance & Operations
Chris Caramalis, VP-Finance **Terri Cunningham**, VP-Managing Editor **Stephanie Fierman**, Sr.VP-Sales & Marketing **Alison Gill**, VP-Manufacturing
Rich Johnson, VP-Book Trade Sales **Hank Kanalz**, VP-General Manager, WildStorm **Lillian Laserson**, Sr.VP & General Counsel
Jim Lee, Editorial Director-WildStorm **Paula Lowitt**, Sr.VP-Business & Legal Affairs **David McKillips**, VP-Advertising & Custom Publishing
Gregory Noveck, Sr.VP-Creative Affairs **Cheryl Rubin**, Sr.VP-Brand Management **Bob Wayne**, VP-Sales

THE QUITTER
Published by DC Comics, 1700 Broadway, New York, NY 10019.
Copyright © 2005 by Harvey Pekar and Dean Haspiel. All Rights Reserved.
All characters featured in this publication, the distinctive likenesses thereof
and related elements are trademarks of Harvey Pekar and Dean Haspiel.
VERTIGO is a trademark of DC Comics.
HC ISBN: 1-4012-0399-X
SC ISBN: 1-4012-0400-7
Printed in Canada
DC Comics, a Warner Bros.
Entertainment Company.
Cover art by Dean Haspiel
Cover color by Lee Loughridge.

To Joyce
— *HARVEY PEKAR*

To my brother, Mike Haspiel,
who is no quitter.
— *DEAN HASPIEL*

Dean Haspiel would like to thank:
Michel Fiffe, John Scott Lucas, Josh Neufeld, and Sarah Butterworth.

I WAS BORN IN CLEVELAND, OHIO, ON OCTOBER 8, 1939, FIVE WEEKS AFTER WORLD WAR II STARTED.

FOR WHAT THAT'S WORTH TO ANYONE.

MY PARENTS WERE BORN IN SHTETLS AROUND BIALYSTOK, POLAND.

MY MOTHER CAME TO CLEVELAND IN THE 1920'S, BUT SHE WENT BACK TO POLAND IN 1935 FOR A TRIP WHERE SHE MET MY FATHER, AND THEY WERE MARRIED SOON AFTER, AND MOVED BACK TO CLEVELAND.

○ BIALYSTOK

POLAND

○ CLEVELAND

OHIO

MY MOTHER'S BROTHER IN-LAW OWNED A SMALL GROCERY STORE ON KINSMAN AVE., IN THE MT. PLEASANT SECTION OF CLEVELAND, WHERE MY FATHER STARTED WORKING.

AFTER A WHILE HE BOUGHT THE STORE AND MY MOTHER AND FATHER RAN IT AS A MOM 'N' POP GROCERY TILL THEY RETIRED IN THE LATE 1960'S.

THE MT. PLEASANT AREA, WHEN THEY MOVED THERE, WAS A WORKING CLASS JEWISH-ITALIAN NEIGHBORHOOD. THEY LIVED IN A TWO-FLAT OR DOUBLE HOUSE, TYPICAL OF THE AREA, WITH MY UNCLE AND AUNT AND THEIR THREE KIDS, ALL OF WHOM WERE BORN IN POLAND, OCCUPYING THE OTHER FLAT.

I LOOKED TO MY MALE COUSIN MORT AS A ROLE MODEL. HE WAS ABOUT TWELVE YEARS OLDER THAN ME.

FROM THE LATE 1930'S TO THE MID 1940'S MY NEIGHBORHOOD WAS CHANGING RAPIDLY FROM WHITE TO BLACK, AND BY 1946, I WAS ABOUT THE ONLY WHITE KID MY AGE LIVING ON MY STREET.

THE BLACK KIDS HAD A NICKNAME FOR ME, "WHITE CRACKER."

IT SEEMED THAT EVERY DAY I CAME HOME FROM SCHOOL, I HAD TO FIGHT THROUGH A BUNCH OF THEM. I HAD NO FRIENDS, AND FELT TOTALLY ALIENATED. I STARTED TO THINK OF MYSELF AS RACIALLY INFERIOR.

MY PARENTS COULD GIVE ME NO HELPFUL SUGGESTIONS. MY MOTHER, A COMMUNIST SYMPATHIZER (SHE SUBSCRIBED TO THE DAILY WORKER), KEPT TELLING ME HOW AFRICAN AMERICANS AND JEWS SHOULD STICK TOGETHER, SINCE BOTH WERE PERSECUTED MINORITIES.

I DIDN'T UNDERSTAND, MEANWHILE, WHY BLACKS, WHOM I'D NEVER HURT, SHOULD GANG UP ON ME.

YOU'VE GOT TO REMEMBER HOW MUCH WE HAVE IN COMMON.

I WANTED TO LOOK TO MY FATHER FOR GUIDANCE, BUT MY FATHER WORKED SO MANY HOURS A WEEK IN THE GROCERY THAT HE HAD NO TIME FOR ME.

BESIDES, HE WANTED TO BRING ME UP LIKE I WAS LIVING IN A POLISH SHTETL. HE HAD NO USE FOR, OR INTEREST IN, AMERICAN CULTURE.

HE STUDIED TALMUD IN THE SMALL AMOUNT OF SPARE TIME HE HAD AND LISTENED TO RECORDS BY THE GREAT CANTORS, KUSSEVITSKY, ROSENBLATT, SIROTA.

WHEN I WAS SIX YEARS OLD, I WAS PLACED IN HEBREW SCHOOL, WHICH I ATTENDED FOUR EVENINGS A WEEK FOR YEARS, UNTIL MY BAR MITZVAH. I HATED HEBREW SCHOOL, BUT I HAD TO GO.

ALEPH, BEIS, GIMMEL. ETC. ETC.

ONE DAY, I LEARNED JUST HOW LITTLE MY PARENTS UNDERSTOOD MY SITUATION. DURING ONE OF MY MANY FIGHTS WITH A GROUP OF BLACK KIDS, MY HAT WAS STOLEN.

I TOLD MY MOTHER ABOUT IT AND ASKED WHAT I SHOULD DO. SHE TOLD ME TO REPORT THE HAT'S THEFT TO THE TEACHER OF THE PUPIL WHO'D STOLEN IT.

BUT MA, THAT'LL JUST GET HIM MADDER AT ME AND HE'LL GET MORE KIDS AFTER ME!

NEVER MIND, YOU DO IT!

THE NEXT DAY, I REPORTED THE STUDENT. THAT EVENING AFTER SCHOOL, I FOUND MYSELF CONFRONTED WITH TWICE AS MANY KIDS TO FIGHT.

AT THAT POINT, I DECIDED THERE WAS NO POINT GOING TO MY PARENTS FOR ADVICE. THEY DIDN'T UNDERSTAND HOW AMERICA WORKED.

THEY GOT ALONG WITH OLDER BLACK PEOPLE THEMSELVES, AND DIDN'T UNDERSTAND THAT RACE RELATIONS IN THE U.S. WERE POISONOUS.

LORED
→
HITE
←

COLORED

THAT AFTER MAKING UNPROVOKED ATTACKS AGAINST BLACKS FOR SO LONG...

...WHITE PEOPLE WERE FINALLY BEING SUBJECTED TO UNPROVOKED ATTACKS BY BLACKS.

WHEN I WAS SIX, MY BROTHER ALLEN WAS BORN. I WAS EXCITED ABOUT THIS, BECAUSE I THOUGHT MY SIBLING WOULD BE MY FRIEND.

AT THIS TIME, I HAD NO INTEREST IN SPORTS, BUT I HEARD THE KIDS IN SCHOOL TALKING ABOUT A BOXING MATCH COMING UP IN CLEVELAND BETWEEN THE GREAT SUGAR RAY ROBINSON AND THE RELATIVELY UNHEARD-OF JEWISH MIDDLEWEIGHT, ARTIE LEVINE.

LEVINE KNOCKED ROBINSON DOWN AND WAS ROBBED OF A K.O. BY THE REFEREE, WHO GAVE SUGAR RAY A LONG COUNT. THE JEWISH KIDS IN SCHOOL WERE BURSTING WITH PRIDE FOR LEVINE, AND I COULDN'T HELP FEELING GOOD ABOUT HIM, TOO.

BUT I SHOULD'VE REALIZED THAT IT WOULD TAKE YEARS FOR MY BROTHER TO BE A COMPANION OF MINE.

HE CAN'T TALK. HE DOESN'T KNOW MY NAME. HOW COULD I HAVE BEEN SO STUPID TO THINK HE'D BE MY FRIEND RIGHT AWAY?

WITH VIRTUALLY NO WHITE PEOPLE LIVING IN OUR IMMEDIATE VICINITY, MY PARENTS DECIDED TO MOVE. THEY WANTED TO BRING ME UP IN A JEWISH ENVIRONMENT. INITIALLY, I THOUGHT THAT WOULD BE GREAT. I WOULDN'T HAVE TO BE THE PARIAH OF THE NEIGHBORHOOD ANYMORE. THAT'S WHAT I THOUGHT, ANYWAY.

OH, TO A JEWISH NEIGHBORHOOD? THAT'LL BE NICE.

I LEARNED WE WERE GOING TO BE MOVING TO A SUBURB CALLED SHAKER HEIGHTS, JUST INSIDE THE CITY LIMITS. SHAKER HEIGHTS WAS RENOWNED THROUGHOUT THE NATION AS A WEALTHY SUBURB, ALTHOUGH THE PART WE LIVED IN LOOKED LIKE MT. PLEASANT, WITH ITS DOUBLE HOUSES. MY AUNT, UNCLE AND COUSINS WOULD BE LIVING UPSTAIRS, AS THEY DID IN THE OTHER HOUSE.

I HAD ALWAYS HAD GOOD RELATIONS WITH MY COUSINS, EVEN THOUGH THEY WERE TOO OLD FOR ME TO HANG OUT WITH.

THE DAY CAME WHEN I WAS SUPPOSED TO MOVE. MY FATHER WAS SUPPOSED TO PICK ME UP IN HIS TRUCK, AT SCHOOL DURING LUNCH HOUR. WE DIDN'T HAVE A CAR, BUT WHEN MY FATHER CAME TO TAKE ME TO THE NEW PLACE, I WAS STANDING WITH SOME OTHER KIDS AND I WAS SUDDENLY EMBARRASSED BY HIM.

HERSCHEL,* COME ON, VE GOTTA GO.

*HERSCHEL WAS MY YIDDISH NAME.

I WAS ASHAMED OF HIS JEWISH ACCENT, HIS OLD-FASHIONED WORK CLOTHES, BY HIS OLD TRUCK. SO, WHEN HE CAME AFTER ME, I RAN AWAY FROM HIM AND THE KIDS THAT WERE STANDING NEAR ME.

HERSCHEL, VERE ARE YOU GOINK?

FORTUNATELY, MY FATHER DIDN'T REALIZE I WAS EMBARRASSED BY HIM. HE THOUGHT I WAS JUST PLAYING A GAME. SO HE FOLLOWED ME, SMILING, UNTIL WE WERE SEVERAL HOUSES AWAY FROM THE OTHER KIDS. I WENT BACK TO THE TRUCK, WHICH WAS ON THE OTHER SIDE OF THE STREET FROM THE KIDS, WITH HIM, SO THEY DIDN'T PAY ATTENTION TO US.

WE DROVE TO THE NEW PLACE WITH ME MARVELING OVER MY LUCK THAT MY FATHER DIDN'T RECOGNIZE THAT I WAS ASHAMED OF HIM, AND AMAZED THAT HE EXHIBITED A SENSE OF HUMOR, WHICH I HADN'T SEEN HIM EXPRESS BEFORE.

ARE WE GETTING CLOSER?

POOTY SOON WE'LL BE THERE.

I LOOKED AROUND AT THE RESIDENTS OF THE STREET. THEY SEEMED TO BE MOSTLY JEWS AND ITALIANS.

MAYBE I'LL BE ABLE TO GET A NEW START HERE.

I DIDN'T HAVE ANY TROUBLE AT MY NEW SCHOOL; I GOT ALONG WITHOUT OVERT HOSTILITY AND MY GRADES WERE GOOD.

HOWEVER, PLEASANT AS RELATIONS WITH MY NEW SCHOOLMATES WERE, I DID NOT MAKE ANYTHING LIKE A PERMANENT FRIEND.

WHEN SUMMER VACATION CAME, THINGS GOT WORSE. I MOSTLY STAYED ON MY OWN STREET, AND THE BOYS THAT LIVED THERE WOULDN'T SPEAK TO ME. AT LEAST THE BLACK KIDS WHO LIVED IN CLEVELAND WOULD COMMUNICATE WITH ME, BUT THE NEW NEIGHBORHOOD ACTED AS IF I DIDN'T EXIST.

THIS STATE OF AFFAIRS LASTED THROUGH MOST OF THE SUMMER. FINALLY, IN AUGUST, I GOT INTO A HEATED ARGUMENT WITH ONE OF THE BOYS ON THE BLOCK. IT DREW A CROWD AND I BEGAN TO FIGHT WITH HIM.

I WON THE FIGHT WITH EASE, TO MY SURPRISE.

I GOT INTO A FIGHT WITH A BOY MY OWN AGE ON THE STREET JUST A FEW MINUTES LATER AND WON THAT ONE, TOO.

THIS AMAZED ME, SINCE I HADN'T WON ANY FIGHTS OF CONSEQUENCE BEFORE THIS.

HOWEVER, I REFLECTED THAT MY FIGHTS IN THE OLD NEIGHBORHOOD WERE AGAINST SEVERAL GUYS AT ONCE, MANY OF WHOM WERE OLDER THAN ME. I'D HAD ALMOST NO EXPERIENCE FIGHTING ONE AGAINST ONE.

IT OCCURRED TO ME THAT MAYBE I WAS A GOOD FIGHTER WHEN I ONLY FOUGHT ONE BOY AT A TIME. IN ANY EVENT, I WAS AMAZED BY MY FEATS AND WAS RELUCTANTLY ADMITTED INTO THE CLIQUE OF KIDS ON HIS STREET.

YOU COULD PLAY BASEBALL WITH US.

I'D LIKE THAT. I'VE NEVER PLAYED BASEBALL BEFORE.

HOWEVER, FOR THE MOST PART, THE KIDS ON THE STREET HAD AN ON-AND-OFF RELATIONSHIP WITH ME. WE SOMETIMES WENT MONTHS WITHOUT SPEAKING. I NEVER UNDERSTOOD WHY, BECAUSE I GOT ON WELL WITH THE KIDS ON OTHER STREETS AND LATER PLAYED FREQUENTLY WITH THEM.

STILL, THESE QUARRELS, FOLLOWED BY PERIODS OF COMMUNICATION, BOTHERED ME. I TOLD MY MOTHER ABOUT ONE OF THE LATEST HASSLES I'D HAD WITH THESE KIDS.

THEY WON'T TALK TO ME. BUT MA, I'M RIGHT AND THEY'RE WRONG ABOUT THIS SITUATION.

MAYBE YOU COULD APOLOGIZE TO THEM.

APOLOGIZE? BUT I TOLD YOU, I'M SURE I'M RIGHT. I'M NOT GOING TO APOLOGIZE WHEN I THINK I'M RIGHT.

SOMETIMES IT DOESN'T MATTER IF YOU'RE RIGHT OR NOT AS LONG AS YOU GET ALONG WITH YOUR FRIENDS.

THIS WILLINGNESS OF MY MOTHER FOR ME TO COMPROMISE OVER THE TRUTH SHOCKED ME. HERE SHE'D BEEN IN FAVOR OF HENRY WALLACE, THE PROGRESSIVE AND COMMUNIST PARTY CANDIDATE FOR PRESIDENT IN 1948, WHO, BELIEVE ME, WAS DEMONIZED BY THE PRESS ALL OVER THE COUNTRY, AND SHE WANTS ME TO COMPROMISE MY PRINCIPLES.

FOR PRESIDENT

HENRY A. WALLACE

SHE EVEN HAD ME PASS OUT LEAFLETS BACKING WALLACE IN THE NEIGHBORHOOD.

WHY WOULD SHE WANT ME TO GIVE UP JUST BECAUSE I WAS IN THE MINORITY?

YOU DON'T HAVE TO GET YOUR WAY ALL THE TIME.

HOW CAN SHE BACK WALLACE AND TELL ME TO GIVE UP WHAT I BELIEVE IN BECAUSE IT'S NOT POPULAR? WHAT MAKES HER LIKE THAT?

HMM. OTHER PEOPLE IN THE FAMILY BACK WALLACE, TOO. THE PEOPLE CLOSEST TO HER BACK HIM, SO SHE'S GOT SUPPORT THERE.

BUT, ON THE OTHER HAND, SHE HAS AN INFERIORITY COMPLEX. SHE'S VERY EMBARRASSED BECAUSE SHE'S SO SHORT, AND MY AUNTS AND UNCLES TEASE HER BECAUSE SHE'S THE YOUNGEST KID IN HER FAMILY. WHEN SHE HAS THEIR SUPPORT ON WALLACE, SHE DOESN'T CARE ABOUT WHAT OTHERS THINK.

BUT SHE'S INSECURE. WHEN SHE SEES THE KIDS ON THE BLOCK AGAINST ME, SHE THINKS I'M BEING STUBBORN, BECAUSE I HAVE NO BACKING.

I WONDER IF SHE REALIZES THAT IT WOULD MEAN SOMETHING FOR HER TO BACK ME UP. PROBABLY NOT.

SO, ONCE AGAIN, I GO MY OWN WAY, BECAUSE I WAS BORN IN AMERICA AND MY WAYS SEEM ALIEN TO HER, JUST LIKE HERS SEEM ALIEN TO ME.

AT THE AGE OF TEN, I STARTED WORKING FOR MY PARENTS ON SATURDAYS IN THEIR STORE, WHICH WAS STILL A SHORT BUS RIDE FROM MY HOUSE.

AT FIRST I FELT PROUD TO BE WORKING AT A JOB AT SUCH A YOUNG AGE. IT WAS LIKE I WAS MORE GROWN-UP THAN MY PEERS.

IT WAS THEN THAT I GOT AN IDEA OF THE HARD WORK MY PARENTS DID. KEEPING THE STORE OPEN SEVEN DAYS A WEEK, FROM JUST AFTER DAWN TO SEVEN IN THE EVENING, OR, ON SUNDAY NIGHTS, 8:30.

MY FATHER WOULD GET UP AT 4:00 IN THE MORNING TO GO DOWN TO THE MARKET AND GET PRODUCE FOR HIS STORE. HE DID NOT CARRY REFRIGERATED PRODUCTS (MEAT, FRESH MILK), OR CIGARETTES OR WINE OR BEER. I GUESS HE FIGURED HE WAS MAKING A LIVING SELLING WHAT HE WAS SELLING, SO THAT'S ALL HE NEEDED.

HE'D BRING THE TRUCK TO THE STORE, UNLOAD IT, AND OPEN FOR BUSINESS. MY MOM MET HIM AT ABOUT 7:30 OR 8:00 AM, WORKED WITH HIM AND RELIEVED HIM FOR LUNCH.

GO GET SOMETHING TO EAT, SHOLEM.

THEN THEY WORKED TOGETHER UNTIL THE EVENING AND WENT HOME. MY MOTHER COOKED DINNER FOR THE FAMILY, EVERYBODY STAYED UP FOR A WHILE, THEN WE'D GO TO BED EARLY FOR THE SAME KIND OF DAY TOMORROW.

MY PARENTS' WORK ETHIC AMAZED ME. HOW COULD THEY PUT IN SUCH LONG HOURS, DAY AFTER DAY?

PART OF THE REASON WAS TO KEEP THE FAMILY GOING--TO KEEP ME GOING. I REALIZED THAT, ALTHOUGH WE HAD DIFFERENT VALUES DERIVED FROM DIFFERENT CULTURES AND WOULDN'T AGREE ON CERTAIN ISSUES, THEY WERE GOOD PEOPLE, INCREDIBLE PEOPLE, AND I LOVED AND RESPECTED THEM.

FOR THE NEXT FEW YEARS I FLOURISHED IN MY ELEMENTARY SCHOOL. I MAINTAINED MY GOOD GRADES WITHOUT TRYING TOO HARD, HELPED BY MY NEAR PHOTOGRAPHIC MEMORY. (SORRY FOR MY BRAGGING, BUT I USED TO HAVE A TREMENDOUS MEMORY.)

AND WITH THE OTHER KIDS ACCEPTING ME, I GOT INTO SPORTS AND FOUND THAT I WAS, BY THE STANDARDS OF MY SCHOOL, A GOOD ATHLETE.

IN FACT, NOT ONLY DID I PLAY A LOT OF BASKETBALL, FOOTBALL AND BASEBALL, I BOUGHT, READ AND COLLECTED A LOT OF SPORTS PUBLICATIONS. YEAH, I HAD A HUGE STASH OF SPORTS STUFF AT ONE TIME. I HAD A SCHOLARLY INTEREST IN IT, MEMORIZED STATISTICS.

IN FACT, MY INTEREST IN SPORTS MAYBE WENT TOO FAR. FOR SEVERAL YEARS PRIOR TO IT, I'D BEEN A BIG READER AND SAVED COMIC BOOKS, WITH STACKS OF THEM ALL OVER THE PLACE. AFTER I GOT TIRED OF THEM AS THEY BECAME TOO FORMULAIC FOR ME, I WAS A VORACIOUS READER OF NOVELS FOR YOUNG PEOPLE. EVEN THEN, I WAS OBSESSIVE-COMPULSIVE.

WHERE DID I PUT THAT *PLASTIC MAN* COMIC?

ANYWAY, I BECAME MORE OUTGOING AT SCHOOL, EVEN TURNING INTO THE CLASS CLOWN.

BUT MAYBE THE MAIN THING WAS THAT IN THE YEARS SINCE I MOVED I DEVELOPED MORE CONFIDENCE BY BEATING UP A NUMBER OF OTHER BOYS.

THIS WAS THE KEY TO MY EGO. I KNEW I COULD FIGHT NOW, AND DIDN'T TAKE SHIT FROM ANYONE.

I BECAME RATHER FANATICAL ABOUT FIGHTING AND SPORTS, BECAUSE SO MUCH OF MY SELF-IMAGE DEPENDED ON THEM.

IF I DIDN'T THINK I COULD GET PRAISE FROM PARTICIPATING IN A SPORT, I'D REFUSE TO PLAY.

IN THE FIFTH GRADE, I QUIT A HARDBALL TEAM ON WHICH I WAS A STARTER BECAUSE I COULDN'T HIT FAST PITCHING WELL ENOUGH.

IT'S NOT THAT I WAS TERRIBLE. I WAS AN OKAY BALLPLAYER, BUT WHEN I FIGURED I WASN'T GOING TO BE A STAR, I OBSESSED ABOUT IT. FROM BEING A NEIGHBORHOOD NOBODY, I WENT TO BEING A NEIGHBORHOOD STAR. ONLY THINKING OF MYSELF IN THIS WAY MADE ME FEEL CALM.

WHAT AM I GONNA DO? WHAT AM I GONNA DO?

MY FAVORITE SPORT WAS TACKLE FOOTBALL, AND I WAS THOUGHT OF AS THE BEST TACKLE FOOTBALL PLAYER IN MY ELEMENTARY SCHOOL.

I HAD TO BE THOUGHT OF AS THE BEST IN SOMETHING.

SO, AFTER BEING WHAT I CONSIDERED A STAR IN ELEMENTARY SCHOOL, I WENT INTO THE SEVENTH GRADE, JUNIOR HIGH SCHOOL. THERE WERE A LOT MORE KIDS IN MY GRADE, AND A LOT MORE COMPETITION.

I COULDN'T GO OUT FOR FOOTBALL IN THE SEVENTH GRADE BECAUSE I STILL HAD TO STUDY FOR MY BAR MITZVAH AFTER SCHOOL.

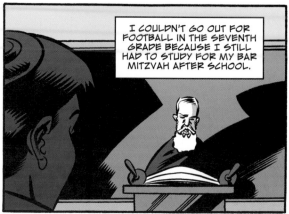

BOY, THAT WAS SCARY. JUST BEFORE I STARTED OUT, MY FATHER CHECKED ME ON MY HEBREW. HE GOT REAL UPSET WITH ME, THOUGHT I WAS TERRIBLE.

HERSCHEL, I COULDN'T BELIEVE YOU'RE SO BAD.

BUT I BUCKLED DOWN TO WORK, BOY. I DIDN'T WANT TO EMBARRASS HIM.

VA YOMER LO

WHEN IT CAME TIME FOR ME TO DO THE CEREMONY, I DID IT IN MY FATHER'S ORTHODOX SYNAGOGUE. A BUNCH OF HIS POLISH FRIENDS WERE THERE. LET ME TELL YOU, THEY WERE A TOUGH AUDIENCE.

I WAS NERVOUS.

BUT I WAS READY, TOO. ALL THAT PRACTICING SHOWED UP. I THINK I WAS PRACTICALLY FLAWLESS.

HERSCHEL, YOU DID A VERY FINE JOB. IF ONLY YOUR GRANDFATHER HAD BEEN ALIVE TO SEE YOU.

IT WAS SO STRANGE. HE FELT SO PROUD OF ME, SO CLOSE TO ME, FOR THAT SMALL AMOUNT OF TIME IN THE SYNAGOGUE, AND THEN, BOOM, WE WENT OUR SEPARATE WAYS, WITH PRACTICALLY NO COMMUNICATION BETWEEN US. WE HAD SO LITTLE IN COMMON. HE HAD SO LITTLE INTEREST IN THE THINGS I DID WELL. SPORTS, HE CONSIDERED A COMPLETE WASTE.

ANOTHER PROBLEM I HAD WHEN I ENTERED JUNIOR HIGH SCHOOL WAS GIRLS. GUYS WERE STARTING TO GO OUT WITH THEM IN THE SEVENTH GRADE, AND I WAS STRONGLY SEXUALLY ATTRACTED TO THEM, BUT I WAS AFRAID TO ASK THEM OUT.

ER, UHH...

YES?

NEVER MIND.

IT'S HARD TO SAY WHY I WAS SO SCARED TO DATE--IT INVOLVED A VARIETY OF THINGS. AT FIRST, ALL THE SOCIAL EVENTS WE WENT TO WERE DANCES, AND I, EMBARRASSINGLY, DIDN'T KNOW HOW TO DANCE.

THEN PART OF IT WAS CLASS. A LOT OF THE GIRLS I LIKED CAME FROM RICHER HOMES THAN ME, AND I FELT LIKE THEY KIND OF LOOKED DOWN THEIR NOSES AT ME.

IT DIDN'T GET ANY BETTER A FEW YEARS LATER IN HIGH SCHOOL, WHEN MOST OF THE DATING WAS DONE WITH CARS. I COULDN'T DRIVE AND DIDN'T GET A LICENSE 'TIL I WAS EIGHTEEN.

I DIDN'T WANT TO TAKE GIRLS ON DATES ON BUSES, SO I ACTUALLY DIDN'T START DATING 'TIL I HAD GRADUATED FROM HIGH SCHOOL, AT EIGHTEEN.

THAT MESSED UP MY CONFIDENCE FOR A LONG TIME. I REALLY FELT LIKE A CREEP. PLUS, I WAS GOING THROUGH A LOT OF CHANGES IN THOSE DAYS, AND HAVING A NICE GIRLFRIEND FOR A WHILE MIGHT'VE MADE MY LOAD A LITTLE EASIER TO CARRY. MAYBE SHE WOULD HAVE BEEN A SYMPATHETIC LISTENER.

THE YEAR I MISSED GOING OUT FOR FOOTBALL MIGHT HAVE HANDICAPPED ME IN THE EIGHTH GRADE, WHEN I FINALLY DID GO OUT, BECAUSE I MISSED OUT ON SOME ORGANIZATIONAL STUFF.

I INTENDED TO GO OUT FOR FULLBACK, BUT WHILE WATCHING THE OTHER KIDS WORK OUT, I DECIDED MAYBE THE COMPETITION WAS TOO STIFF, AND SWITCHED TO GUARD, WHICH IS A SIMPLER POSITION AND WHERE I WAS BOUND TO STAND OUT (I THOUGHT). BUT EIGHTH GRADE FOOTBALL PROVED TO BE A REAL DISASTER.

FOR ONE THING, MY COACH WAS A GUY WHO HAD ME FOR SEVENTH GRADE SCIENCE AND CONSIDERED ME A REAL GOOF-OFF. HE COULDN'T TAKE ME SERIOUSLY AS AN ATHLETE AND IN ONE SCRIMMAGE DIDN'T PLAY ME AT ALL, EVEN THOUGH ALL THE KIDS WERE YELLING THAT HE'D FORGOTTEN TO PUT ME IN.

COACH, HARVEY HASN'T PLAYED YET.

WHEN THE TIME CAME TO COMPETE FOR POSITIONS, THE COACH WOULD ONLY GIVE ME A CHANCE TO PLAY ON DEFENSE, NOT OFFENSE. NEVERTHELESS, I WOUND UP PLAYING DEFENSIVE STARTING GUARD.

I DID A REAL GOOD JOB, I THINK, OVER THE FIRST SEVERAL GAMES, BUT FOR SOME REASON, THE COACH PULLED ME OUT AND REPLACED ME WITH SOME GUY NAMED BUCK, WHO WAS A SPASTIC. THE GUY WAS MISSING TACKLES ALL OVER THE FIELD AND THE COACH WOULDN'T PUT ME BACK.

I COULDN'T FIGURE OUT WHY THE COACH WOULDN'T USE ME ANY-MORE, EXCEPT THAT MAYBE HE WAS GETTING BACK AT ME FOR SCREWING AROUND IN HIS CLASS LAST YEAR.

SO I QUIT THE TEAM. THIS DISMAYED SOME OF MY TEAMMATES, WHO URGED ME TO COME BACK, AS BUCK WAS DOING SO BADLY. BUT AT THAT TIME I DIDN'T WANT TO THINK ABOUT PLAYING FOOTBALL. I FIGURED I WAS BEING MESSED OVER BY FORCES I COULDN'T CONTROL AND PUT MY DREAMS OF BEING A FOOTBALL STAR ON HOLD.

HARVEY, AIN'T YA COMING BACK?

NOT THIS YEAR.

THE NEXT YEAR, I WENT OUT FOR FOOTBALL AGAIN, BUT WAS ASSIGNED THE SAME COACH, WHO AGAIN WOULDN'T EVEN CONSIDER USING ME ON OFFENSE. HOWEVER, I STARTED ON DEFENSE AND HAD A GOOD SEASON ALL YEAR LONG.

THIS TIME, I DIDN'T HAVE ANY "BUCK-LIKE" SURPRISES PULLED ON ME.

AT THE END OF THE SEASON, I FELT THAT DESPITE MY OWN COACH MESSING WITH ME, THE OTHER COACHES THOUGHT I WAS GOOD, AND I HAD REASON TO BELIEVE ONE RECOMMENDED ME AS ONE OF THE MOST PROM-ISING PROSPECTS FOR NEXT YEAR'S JUNIOR VARSITY.

HARVEY, HOW DO YOU SPELL YOUR LAST NAME?

I BEGAN WORKING OUT FOR THE HIGH SCHOOL JUNIOR VARSITY FOOTBALL TEAM IN THE SUMMER BEFORE I ENTERED HIGH SCHOOL (10TH GRADE).

NOW I THOUGHT I HAD AN OPEN SHOT AT WINNING A STARTING POSITION. NONE OF MY COACHES HAD ME IN A CLASSROOM OR CONSIDERED ME A GOOF-OFF.

I PERFORMED WELL ON THE BLOCKING SLEDS AND IN SPRINTS.

THERE WAS A PROBLEM THOUGH. ONE OF THE GUYS WHO WOULD GIVE ME MY MAIN COMPETITION AT GUARD GOT SENT OFF TO WORK WITH THE RUNNING BACKS FOR SEVERAL DAYS, DURING WHICH I WAS IMPRESSIVE. WHEN HE CAME BACK, HE WAS INSTALLED IN THE STARTING LINEUP AHEAD OF ME, THOUGH HE'D DONE NO WORK AT GUARD.

IN THE EARLY SCRIMMAGES, I EASILY BEAT THIS GUY WHEN HE WAS LINED UP AGAINST ME.

ONCE, I KNOCKED HIM DOWN AND POINTED AT HIS BODY SO THE COACH REALIZED I WAS BEATING HIM.

Y'SEE! Y'SEE!

BUT THE NEXT DAY I WAS STILL NOT ON THE STARTING TEAM. EVEN AT THIS STAGE IN MY LIFE I WAS DEEPLY DEPRESSED AND PESSIMISTIC.

I FELT THERE WAS A FORCE WORKING AGAINST ME THAT WASN'T ALLOWING COACHES TO GIVE ME A STARTING POSITION NO MATTER HOW BADLY I MAULED MY COMPETITORS.

THE THOUGHT THAT I WOULDN'T BE ABLE TO MAKE THE STARTING SQUADRON NO MATTER WHAT I DID HAUNTED ME, IT TORE AT ME. THE ONLY WAY I COULD GET IT OFF MY BACK WAS TO TAKE THE EXTREME STEP OF QUITTING THE TEAM.

YOU'RE QUITTIN'? BUT YOU JUST GOT STARTED. C'MON, HARVEY.

NAW, THIS THING IS TEARING ME UP. I FEEL NO MATTER HOW GOOD I DO IN ANYTHING, I'M NOT GOING TO GET ANY CREDIT.

THIS, OF COURSE, WAS A HUGE SETBACK TO ME. I WANTED TO BE A FOOTBALL STAR SO BADLY, BUT THE DAY-TO-DAY AGONIZING OVER WHETHER I GOT MY PROPS OR NOT WAS A TORTURE I COULDN'T TAKE.

SINCE I REALIZED I WAS MORE THAN A COMPLETE NOTHING, I CRAVED RECOGNITION AS THE BEST IN ONE FIELD OR ANOTHER. NOW FOOTBALL WAS NOT AN OPTION FOR ME.

WHAT WOULD I HAVE TO DO TO KEEP MY MORALE UP ENOUGH TO AT LEAST BE ABLE TO SHOW UP IN SCHOOL EVERY DAY?

MY MOTHER HAD A LOW OPINION OF HERSELF AND DIDN'T MIND PASSING HER FEELINGS ON TO ME.

I GOT THREE "A'S" ANNA "B" IN SCHOOL, MA.

WHAT DID YOU GET THE "B" IN, HARVEY? YOU HAVE TO PRACTICE, PRACTICE, PRACTICE AND STUDY, STUDY, STUDY, SO YOU WON'T SLIP.

BUT, MA, I'M DOING REALLY WELL IN SCHOOL NOW, AND I'M NOT KILLING MYSELF. I GOT A REAL GOOD MEMORY, SO MAYBE I DON'T HAVE TO WORK AS HARD AS SOME STUDENTS, BUT I DON'T GOOF OFF. I ALWAYS DO MY HOMEWORK.

AND THREE "A'S" ANNA "B" ARE REAL GOOD GRADES.

YES, HARVEY, YOU'RE LUCKY TO HAVE SUCH A GOOD MEMORY, BUT YOU CAN'T ALWAYS RELY ON IT. YOU HAVE TO STUDY AND PRACTICE HARDER.

EVERYBODY DOES. THOSE THAT ARE LAZY FALL BEHIND.

IT'S BAD TO BE LIKE THAT.

YOU CAN'T IMPRESS EVERYBODY AND SOMETIMES, MAYBE THROUGH NO FAULT OF YOUR OWN--

--YOU CAN'T IMPRESS IMPORTANT PEOPLE WHO COULD HAVE A VERY POSITIVE EFFECT ON YOUR LIFE.

BUT EVEN TODAY I CAN'T BE COOL ABOUT IT.

AND THERE ARE LOTS OF PEOPLE LIKE ME.

SO, I DON'T KNOW WHAT TO DO. I REALIZED THAT I OUGHT TO KEEP ON JUST GOING TO SCHOOL AND SEE WHAT CAME UP. MAYBE SOMETHING WOULD.

IT WASN'T AS BAD AS IT'D BEEN WHEN I WAS SIX AND NOBODY REALLY SHOWED ME AFFECTION. NOW I HAD SOME FRIENDS, A FEW OF WHOM THOUGHT HIGHLY OF ME.

WRESTLING WOULD HAVE BEEN A GOOD THING FOR ME TO GET INTO, SINCE I WAS EXTREMELY STRONG FOR MY SIZE.

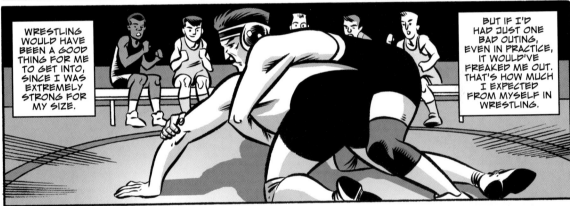

BUT IF I'D HAD JUST ONE BAD OUTING, EVEN IN PRACTICE, IT WOULD'VE FREAKED ME OUT. THAT'S HOW MUCH I EXPECTED FROM MYSELF IN WRESTLING.

SO, I WAS ABOUT FOURTEEN THEN AND I HAD STARTED WORKING MORE IN MY PARENTS' GROCERY, AFTER SCHOOL AS WELL AS SATURDAYS.

HOW MUCH ARE THESE COLLARD GREENS, TODAY?

COLLARDS ARE TWO POUNDS FOR NINE CENTS.

I DIDN'T LIKE WORKING THERE ANYMORE. IT WAS A DRAG.

MY FATHER'S STORE WAS ABLE TO LAST AS LONG AS IT DID BECAUSE THE NEIGHBORHOOD AROUND IT WAS SO BLEAK AND UNLIVELY THAT NO CHAIN GROCERIES LOCATED IN IT. EVEN AT THAT, BUSINESS WAS SLOW, BUT PEOPLE DID SOME OF THEIR SHOPPING THERE.

LIKE, IF THEY JUST NEEDED A FEW THINGS, THEY WOULDN'T WANT TO DRIVE TO ANOTHER AREA TO GET THEM IN A CHAIN STORE.

LEMME HAVE A LOAF OF BREAD AND SOME VELVEETA CHEESE.

I KNEW A LOT OF THE CUSTOMERS WHO CAME IN THERE. THEY'D BEEN GETTING STUFF FROM MY PARENTS' STORE FOR YEARS.

HELLO, MRS. MacDANIEL.

HELLO, LI'L SOL. GIMME THREE POUNDS A' KENTUCKY WONDERS T'START WITH, AND THEN...

THEY WERE MOSTLY OLDER AND HAD LIVED IN THE NEIGHBORHOOD FOR A LONG TIME. THEY KNEW MY PARENTS WERE HONEST AND THAT THEY TRUSTED THE CUSTOMERS ENOUGH TO LET THEM BUY ON CREDIT.

THAT'LL BE $8.17, M'AM.

PUT IT ON THE BOOKS AND I'LL PAY YOU NEXT SATURDAY.

IN SOME CASES, THEY WERE KIND OF INTERESTED IN HOW MY FAMILY WAS GETTING ALONG.

ARE YOU KEEPING YOUR MARKS UP?

YEAH, I GOTTA BETTER THAN "B" AVERAGE.

THAT'S GOOD. YOU'RE A BRIGHT BOY.

AS NICE AS THE CUSTOMERS WERE TO US, WORKING AT THE STORE REALLY DEPRESSED ME.

FOR ONE THING, BUSINESS WAS SLOW. A LOT OF THE TIME, I STOOD AROUND IN THE STORE, ALONE AND IN GLOOM.

SIGH

THE SLOW BUSINESS MADE ME FEEL WE WERE BEING REJECTED BY MOST OF THE NEIGHBORS, WHO DID THEIR SHOPPING IN A CHAIN STORE IN AN ADJACENT NEIGHBORHOOD AND JUST BOUGHT SMALL ORDERS FROM US.

PLUS, THE STORE ITSELF WAS LACKLUSTER. IT NEVER EVEN HAD A NAME.

THERE WAS AN ANCIENT SALADA TEA SIGN ON ONE OF THE WINDOWS, BUT NO NAME.

THE OTHER STORES IN THE NEIGHBORHOOD WERE SMALL LIKE OURS, AND OLD-FASHIONED. NEXT DOOR TO US WAS A BUTCHER SHOP OWNED BY TWO CZECH BROTHERS, CARL AND RUDY. THEY ALSO WORKED IN FACTORIES. THEY WERE NICE GUYS WHO'D BEEN IN THE NEIGHBORHOOD FOR A LONG TIME, TOO.

BUT THE STORE, THE NEIGHBORHOOD, THEY WERE DYING. AND WORKING THERE, I FELT LIKE I WAS DYING TOO. DRYING UP AND DYING.

I TRIED TO GET JOBS AFTER SCHOOL AT OTHER PLACES, BUT COULDN'T FOR A COUPLE OF YEARS.

SORRY, WE'RE NOT HIRING.

SO, AFTER SCHOOL AND ON SATURDAYS, MY UNIVERSE JUST SEEMED LIKE IT WAS DECAYING.

WHAT WAS I GONNA DO TO CHEER MYSELF UP? I HAD QUIT SPORTS, I WAS TOO AFRAID TO ASK GIRLS OUT.

WELL, I FELL INTO SOMETHING THAT KEPT ME GOING--STREET FIGHTING.

I HAD DECIDED LONG AGO THAT THE MOST RESPECTED PEOPLE IN MY TEENAGE WORLD WERE STREET FIGHTERS.

WHY NOT DIRECT MY EFFORTS TOWARDS BECOMING ONE OF THE BEST STREET FIGHTERS IN THE NEIGHBORHOOD?

YEAH!

ACTUALLY, I WAS ALREADY CONSIDERED ONE BY MY PEERS, BUT I WANTED TO GET MORE RECOGNITION IN THIS AREA.

NOW, IN THOSE DAYS, JUST ABOUT ALL FIGHTS THAT TOOK PLACE BETWEEN KIDS WHO WERE, SAY, FOURTEEN AND YOUNGER, AMOUNTED TO WRESTLING MATCHES.

A GUY WHO PUNCHED PEOPLE WITH HIS FISTS WAS KIND OF DANGEROUS--LIKE HE COULD ACTUALLY HURT PEOPLE.

BUT I THOUGHT I WOULD GO ALL THE WAY INTO FIST FIGHTING. I FIGURED I WOULDN'T TRY TO PICK ON OR BULLY PEOPLE I COULD OBVIOUSLY BEAT UP, BUT IF SOMEBODY REALLY PISSED ME OFF, I WAS GONNA SOCK HIM.

ACTUALLY, I FELT KIND OF BAD ABOUT THE FIRST GUY I PUNCHED. HE WAS A NICE GUY AND A GOOD ATHLETE, BUT NOT MEAN ENOUGH TO BE A FIGHTER. WE WERE TALKING. HE WAS BUGGING ME.

SO WHAT I DID, I JUST WOUND UP AND SLUGGED HIM. ONCE WAS ENOUGH.

SOCK

HE QUIT FIGHTING AND REALLY GOT UPSET.

WHAT DID YOU DO THAT FOR? I WASN'T GOING TO HIT YOU. ARE YOU NUTS OR SOMETHING?

I PROBABLY SHOULDN'T HAVE HIT HIM, BUT THERE WERE PEOPLE AROUND AND THEY SAW IT.

HEY, HARVEY, WAY TO GO. I NEVER DID LIKE THAT CHARACTER.

WELL, A WIN IS A WIN.

A WHILE LATER, I SCORED A MORE IMPRESSIVE VICTORY OVER A GUY I REALLY DISLIKED, IN THE BATHROOM OF THE BOYS' LOCKER ROOM.

THIS GUY WAS GERMAN AND HIS PARENTS WERE RUMORED TO BE PRO-NAZI. HE AND I HADN'T GOTTEN ALONG WELL FOR YEARS. I TOOK EXCEPTION TO SOMETHING HE SAID AFTER GYM CLASS.

WHAT'D YOU SAY?

YOU HEARD ME.

YEAH, I HEARD YOU.

HE AIMED A HALF-HEARTED PUNCH AT MY STOMACH, WHICH I BLOCKED.

THEN I REALIZED THIS GAVE ME LICENSE TO RETALIATE, WHICH I DID.

I JUMPED ON HIM AND SOCKED HIM SOME MORE WHEN HE WAS DOWN.

AND LEFT HIM OUT, WITH HIS HEAD NEAR THE URINAL.

LATER...

'AY, HARVEY, I HEARD YOU K.O.'D SCHULTZ AND LEFT HIM WITH HIS HEAD LAYING IN A URINAL.

NICE GOING. S'WHAT HE DESERVES.

HARVEY, I HEARD YOU BEAT UP SCHULTZ SO BAD T'DAY, HE HAD T' GO HOME FROM SCHOOL. NICE GOIN'.

THESE ALL HELPED MY REPUTATION SOME, BUT THE BIG FIGHT OF THE SCHOOL YEAR WAS ME AGAINST NICK LOPINTO, WHICH HAPPENED IN LATE SPRING.

ANGELONE'S

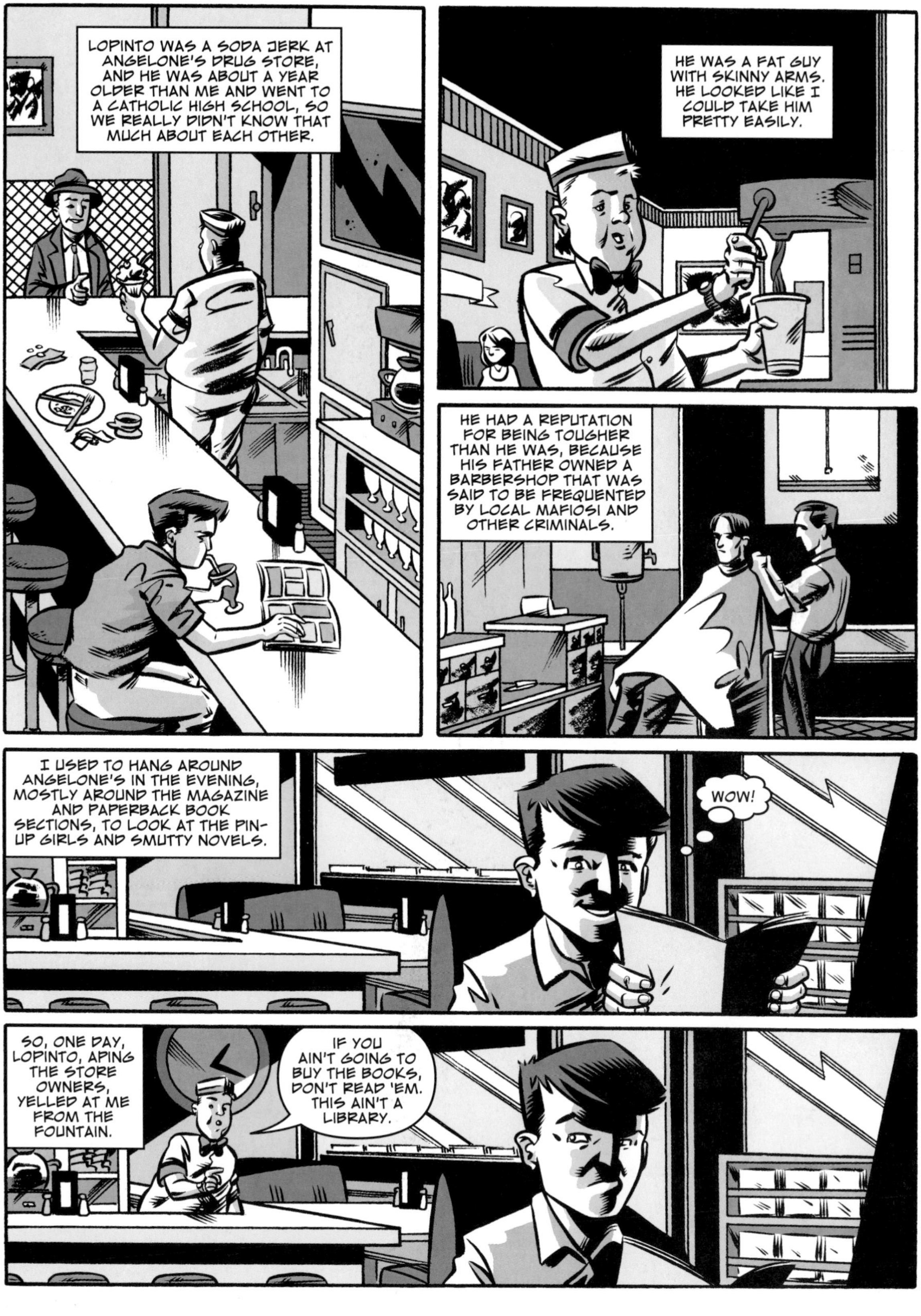
LOPINTO WAS A SODA JERK AT ANGELONE'S DRUG STORE, AND HE WAS ABOUT A YEAR OLDER THAN ME AND WENT TO A CATHOLIC HIGH SCHOOL, SO WE REALLY DIDN'T KNOW THAT MUCH ABOUT EACH OTHER.
HE WAS A FAT GUY WITH SKINNY ARMS. HE LOOKED LIKE I COULD TAKE HIM PRETTY EASILY.
HE HAD A REPUTATION FOR BEING TOUGHER THAN HE WAS, BECAUSE HIS FATHER OWNED A BARBERSHOP THAT WAS SAID TO BE FREQUENTED BY LOCAL MAFIOSI AND OTHER CRIMINALS.
I USED TO HANG AROUND ANGELONE'S IN THE EVENING, MOSTLY AROUND THE MAGAZINE AND PAPERBACK BOOK SECTIONS, TO LOOK AT THE PIN-UP GIRLS AND SMUTTY NOVELS.
WOW!
SO, ONE DAY, LOPINTO, APING THE STORE OWNERS, YELLED AT ME FROM THE FOUNTAIN.
IF YOU AIN'T GOING TO BUY THE BOOKS, DON'T READ 'EM. THIS AIN'T A LIBRARY.

THIS WAS A PERFECT SETUP FOR ME, BECAUSE I FIGURED I COULD FLATTEN THE CLUMSY, UNATHLETIC LOPINTO. LOPINTO, HOWEVER, THOUGHT HE COULD TAKE ME, BECAUSE HE WAS BIGGER. SINCE HE DIDN'T GO TO MY SCHOOL, HE DIDN'T REALIZE I WAS A TOUGH KID, SO I ANSWERED.

MIND YOUR OWN BIZNESS, FATBOY.

HERE'S A CHANCE TO STOMP A GUY WITH A "TOUGH GUY" REPUTATION WHO REALLY ISN'T VERY TOUGH.

'AY, IF I CATCH YOU IN THE STREET, I'LL KILL YOU.

OH, YEAH, WELL I'LL SEE YOU IN THE STREET T'MORROW AFTER WORK.

AS I WALK OUT OF THE STORE, I TELL MY FRIENDS.

I AIN'T SHITTIN' LOPINTO. WHEN HE GETS OFF WORK TOMORROW, I'LL BE WAITIN'.

THE NEXT DAY, I URGED MY BUDDIES IN THE NEIGHBORHOOD TO COME UP TO THE FIGHT WITH ME.

I KNOW I CAN TAKE 'IM.

THEN I WENT UP TO ANGELONE'S WHERE LOPINTO WAS WORKING AND I SAID TO HIM--

I'LL SEE YOU IN THE STREET.

HUH?

LOPINTO HAD PROBABLY FORGOTTEN ABOUT WHAT WAS SAID YESTERDAY.

AT 5:15 I WENT UP TO ANGELONE'S TO MEET LOPINTO, WHO GOT OFF AT 5:30.

THERE WERE SOME GUYS ALREADY WAITING TO SEE THE ACTION.

AAAY, BIG HARV!

GUYS WERE RUNNING INSIDE AND OUTSIDE THE STORE, PRESUMABLY TELLING LOPINTO I'M WAITING. THEN LOPINTO COMES OUT, STILL PUZZLED ABOUT WHAT'S GOING ON.

WHAT'S'IS ALL ABOUT?

YOU SAID IF YOU SAW ME INNA STREET, YOU'D KILL ME. WELL, HERE I AM!

LOPINTO DIDN'T SEEM LIKE HE WAS INTO FIGHTING, BUT THERE WERE ALL THESE GUYS WATCHING, WHAT COULD HE DO? HE SLAPPED ME AND TRIED TO GET ME IN A HEADLOCK. I PUSHED HIM AWAY AND HIT HIM WITH A RIGHT CROSS.

HE SPUN AROUND AND WENT DOWN ON ALL FOURS.

WHEN HE GOT UP, HE WAS ALL COVERED WITH BLOOD ON ONE SIDE OF HIS FACE FROM A BAD EYE CUT.

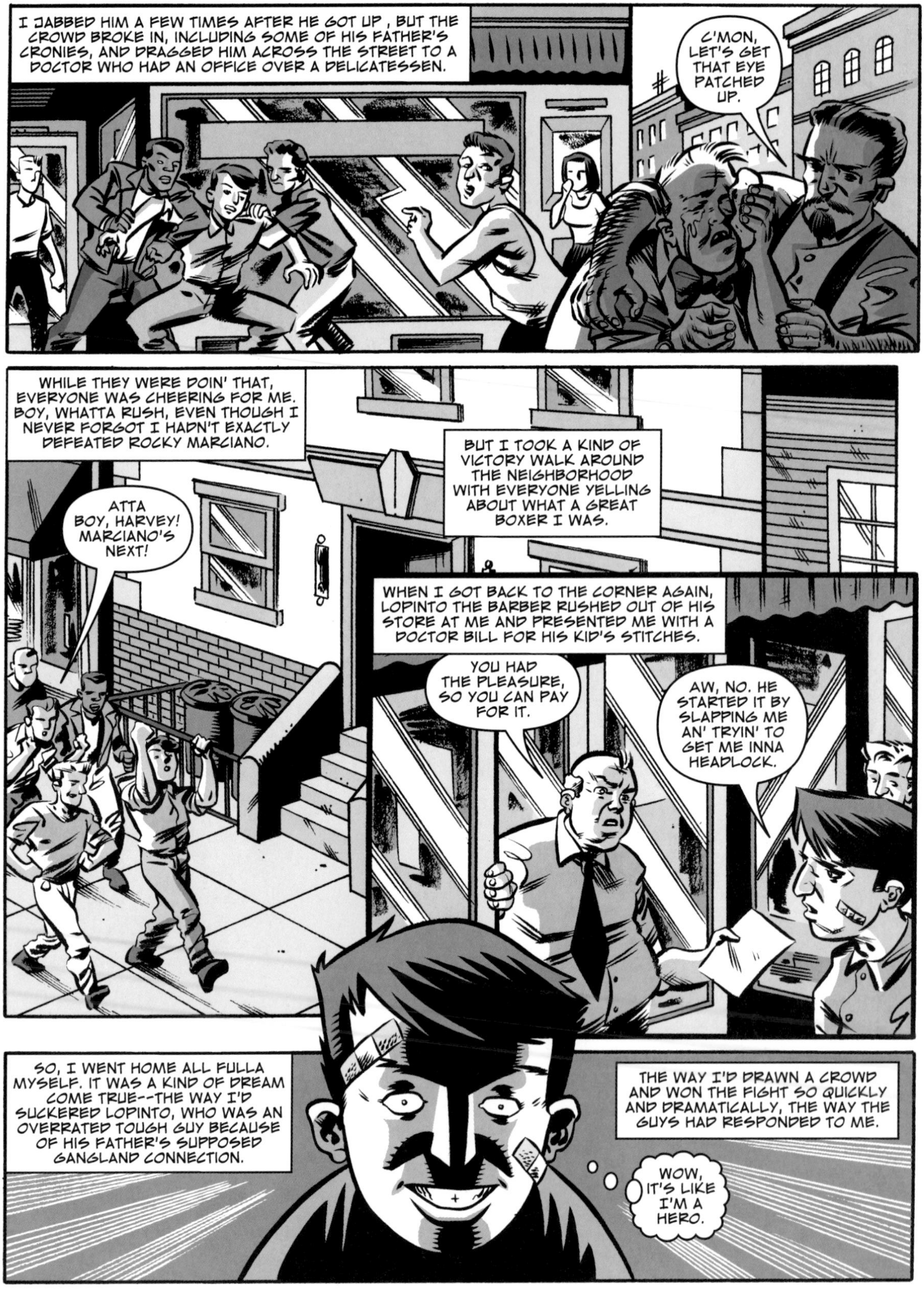

I JABBED HIM A FEW TIMES AFTER HE GOT UP, BUT THE CROWD BROKE IN, INCLUDING SOME OF HIS FATHER'S CRONIES, AND DRAGGED HIM ACROSS THE STREET TO A DOCTOR WHO HAD AN OFFICE OVER A DELICATESSEN.
C'MON, LET'S GET THAT EYE PATCHED UP.
WHILE THEY WERE DOIN' THAT, EVERYONE WAS CHEERING FOR ME. BOY, WHATTA RUSH, EVEN THOUGH I NEVER FORGOT I HADN'T EXACTLY DEFEATED ROCKY MARCIANO.
BUT I TOOK A KIND OF VICTORY WALK AROUND THE NEIGHBORHOOD WITH EVERYONE YELLING ABOUT WHAT A GREAT BOXER I WAS.
ATTA BOY, HARVEY! MARCIANO'S NEXT!
WHEN I GOT BACK TO THE CORNER AGAIN, LOPINTO THE BARBER RUSHED OUT OF HIS STORE AT ME AND PRESENTED ME WITH A DOCTOR BILL FOR HIS KID'S STITCHES.
YOU HAD THE PLEASURE, SO YOU CAN PAY FOR IT.
AW, NO. HE STARTED IT BY SLAPPING ME AN' TRYIN' TO GET ME INNA HEADLOCK.
SO, I WENT HOME ALL FULLA MYSELF. IT WAS A KIND OF DREAM COME TRUE--THE WAY I'D SUCKERED LOPINTO, WHO WAS AN OVERRATED TOUGH GUY BECAUSE OF HIS FATHER'S SUPPOSED GANGLAND CONNECTION.
THE WAY I'D DRAWN A CROWD AND WON THE FIGHT SO QUICKLY AND DRAMATICALLY, THE WAY THE GUYS HAD RESPONDED TO ME.
WOW, IT'S LIKE I'M A HERO.

THE NEXT DAY, I WENT BACK TO SCHOOL. EVERYONE WAS STILL CHEERING ME.

I HEARD YOU KNOCKED THE GUY'S HEAD OFF.

HIS EYE WAS SWOLLEN UP LIKE AN EGG.

FROM THIS EXTRAVAGANZA I HAD PRACTICALLY STAGED MYSELF, I GOT PRETTY MUCH WHAT I WANTED. I WAS CONSIDERED ONE OF THE TOUGHEST GUYS IN SCHOOL, AN OUTRIGHT LEGEND.

AAAY, HARVEY!

HEY, MAN.

THIS WAS GOING TO GET ME A LOT MORE RESPECT AND NOTORIETY, BUT WHEN I THOUGHT ABOUT IT, IT DIDN'T FIGURE TO MAKE THAT MUCH OF A CHANGE IN MY SELF IMAGE. I WAS STILL VERY INSECURE ABOUT EVERYTHING. MY MOTHER HAD ALWAYS TOLD ME TO, "PREPARE FOR THE WORST, SO IF IT HAPPENS, YOU WON'T BE SURPRISED." I BELIEVED HER AND COULDN'T SEE HOW I'D BE ABLE TO MAKE IT IN ADULT LIFE.

I GOT DISCOURAGED ABOUT STUFF SO FAST AND WOULD WALK AWAY FROM A CHALLENGE RATHER THAN CONFRONT IT. FOR EXAMPLE, EARLIER THAT YEAR, I HAD QUIT AN ALGEBRA CLASS WHEN I GOT A LOW GRADE ON A TEST, AND SWITCHED TO GEOGRAPHY CLASS, WHICH WAS ONE I COULD ACE.

ALL I GOTTA DO IS MEMORIZE THE NAMES OF CITIES AND STUFF.

I COULDN'T DO ANYTHING MECHANICAL, WASN'T GOING TO GO TO COLLEGE, BECAUSE COLLEGE WOULD REQUIRE THAT YOU TAKE A MATH CLASS, WHICH I COULDN'T HANDLE. HOW WAS I GOING TO SUPPORT MYSELF?

WHEN I GET OUTTA HIGH SCHOOL, I'LL BE A BASKET CASE!

MAYBE IT WAS TOO EARLY TO START WORRYING ABOUT STUFF LIKE THAT, BUT I DID.

AND I STILL WONDER TODAY HOW I'M GOING TO GET BY THE NEXT SEVERAL YEARS.

AROUND THIS TIME (1955) MY PARENTS MADE THE PLUNGE AND FINALLY BOUGHT A TV SET. AT ONE TIME, BOXING MATCHES WERE SHOWN FOUR NIGHTS A WEEK AND I USED TO WATCH AS MANY OF THEM AS I COULD.

I'D NEVER FOLLOWED THE SPORT CLOSELY, BUT NOW I REALLY GOT INTO IT, EVEN STARTED READING ABOUT IT AND COLLECTING OLD BOXING MAGAZINES AND BOOKS.

WHAT I FOUND OUT, AMONG OTHER THINGS, WAS THAT JEWS WERE VERY ACTIVE AS BOXERS IN THE 1920'S AND 1930'S, INCLUDING A LOT OF FINE FIGHTERS. SOME THAT WERE CHAMPIONS.

THAT KIND OF SURPRISED ME. I DIDN'T KNOW MUCH ABOUT JEWISH BOXERS, BUT THEY GOT INTO THE SPORT WHEN THEY WERE RECENT IMMIGRANTS AND DIDN'T HAVE MUCH MONEY.

THEN GOT OUT IN THE 1940'S WITH THE COMING OF BETTER ECONOMIC OPPORTUNITIES.

THIS INDICATED THAT THEY WEREN'T IN LOVE WITH BOXING, JUST WANTED TO USE IT TO MAKE A LIVING UNTIL SOMETHING BETTER CAME ALONG. STILL, (THIS WAS BEFORE MY ANTI-NATIONALIST BELIEFS HAD SUNK IN), I WAS PROUD OF A LOT OF JEWISH BOXERS, LIKE BENNY LEONARD, CONSIDERED ONE OF THE FINEST LIGHTWEIGHTS OF ALL TIME.

IN THE 11TH AND 12TH GRADES, I WON MORE FIGHTS, BUT THEY WERE NOT THE BIG DEAL THEY USED TO BE FOR ME. FOR ONE THING, I REALLY DIDN'T LIKE BEATING PEOPLE UP THAT MUCH. FOR ANOTHER, I HAD THE RESPECT I WANTED FOR BEING A FIGHTER ALREADY AND HAD LITTLE TO GAIN BY BEATING OTHER GUYS UP.

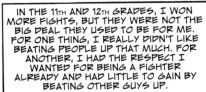

I HAD A FEW GOOD FRIENDS IN THOSE DAYS, MOST OF WHOM DID NOT COME FROM THE UPPER CRUST OF SHAKER HEIGHTS SOCIETY.

THERE WAS LARRY, A POSTAL WORKER'S SON;

BUBBLES, WHOSE MOTHER AND SISTER OWNED A SHOP FOR PRE-SCHOOL KIDS;

LLOYD, WHOSE PARENTS OWNED A SMALL GROCERY LIKE MINE;

AND BOBBY, WHOSE FATHER WAS A SALESMAN (OF WHAT I NEVER FOUND OUT); AND SEVERAL MORE.

WE FELT LIKE WE WERE LOSERS. WE SELDOM, IF EVER, WENT ON DATES. YOU'D THINK THERE WOULD BE AT LEAST ONE GIRL IN THE SCHOOL WHO ADMIRED ME FOR MY TOUGH GUY STATUS, BUT, IF SO, I WAS UNAWARE OF HER.

HEY, UHH...

YEAH?

NEVER MIND.

SO WE WOULD HANG TOGETHER, AND IN OUR MISERY MADE GOOD COMPANY FOR EACH OTHER. WE ALL HAD PRETTY GOOD SENSES OF HUMOR AND COULD GENERALLY CHEER EACH OTHER UP.

SO, THEN I SAID...

THAT'S TELLING 'IM!

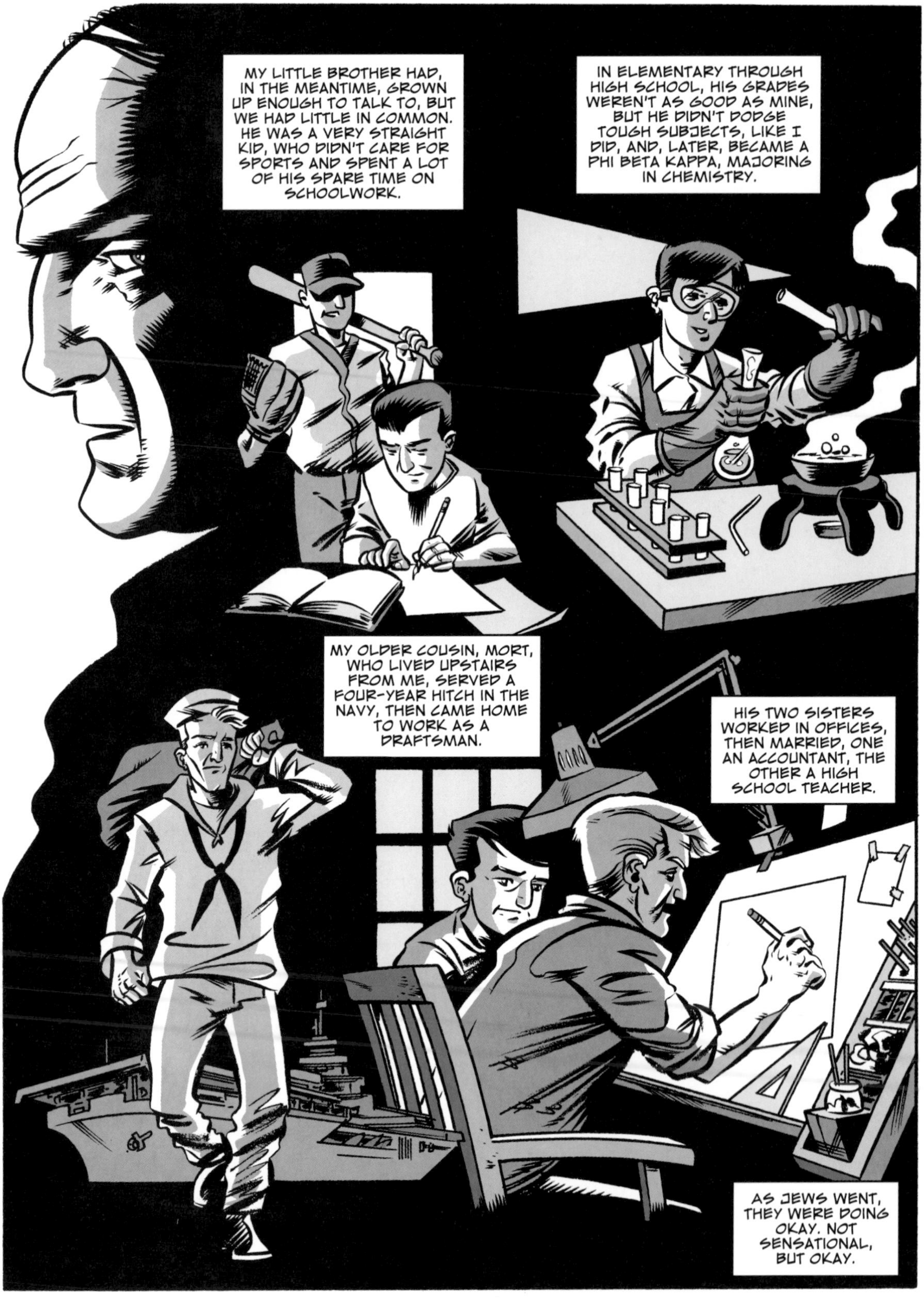
MY LITTLE BROTHER HAD, IN THE MEANTIME, GROWN UP ENOUGH TO TALK TO, BUT WE HAD LITTLE IN COMMON. HE WAS A VERY STRAIGHT KID, WHO DIDN'T CARE FOR SPORTS AND SPENT A LOT OF HIS SPARE TIME ON SCHOOLWORK.
IN ELEMENTARY THROUGH HIGH SCHOOL, HIS GRADES WEREN'T AS GOOD AS MINE, BUT HE DIDN'T DODGE TOUGH SUBJECTS, LIKE I DID, AND, LATER, BECAME A PHI BETA KAPPA, MAJORING IN CHEMISTRY.
MY OLDER COUSIN, MORT, WHO LIVED UPSTAIRS FROM ME, SERVED A FOUR-YEAR HITCH IN THE NAVY, THEN CAME HOME TO WORK AS A DRAFTSMAN.
HIS TWO SISTERS WORKED IN OFFICES, THEN MARRIED, ONE AN ACCOUNTANT, THE OTHER A HIGH SCHOOL TEACHER.
AS JEWS WENT, THEY WERE DOING OKAY. NOT SENSATIONAL, BUT OKAY.

THIS KEY THING HAPPENED TO ME IN AN 11TH GRADE ENGLISH CLASS. I WAS SUPPOSED TO MAKE A SPEECH. I COULD CHOOSE JUST ABOUT ANY SUBJECT, SO WHAT SHOULD THAT SUBJECT BE?

WELL, IT JUST SO HAPPENED THAT I WAS READING ABOUT COLORFUL CHARACTERS, COWBOYS LIKE WYATT EARP.

AND I'D JUST BOUGHT A BOOK ON JAZZMEN, LIKE JELLY ROLL MORTON.

THE JAZZ BOOK PROVED PRETTY INTERESTING TO ME. SO INTERESTING THAT I BOUGHT A 99 CENT LP, CALLED "JAZZ OF TWO DECADES," TO ILLUSTRATE MY SPEECH.

I'M ABOUT TO PLAY AN EXAMPLE OF THE JAZZ STYLE KNOWN AS, "DIXIELAND."

THE SPEECH WAS WELL RECEIVED, AND MY INTEREST IN JAZZ TURNED OUT TO BE MORE THAN TEMPORARY. THE JAZZ ARTISTS DID PROVE TO BE FASCINATING CHARACTERS, BUT I WAS EVEN MORE INTERESTED IN THEIR MUSIC. I LISTENED TO MORE JAZZ AT HOME.

AND I GOT CAUGHT UP IN IT. FORTUNATELY, I HAD A FRIEND A YEAR OLDER THAN ME WHO WAS A SERIOUS JAZZ TRUMPETER. HE TURNED ME ON TO THE MORE MODERN FORMS OF JAZZ, LIKE "BOP" AND A LOT OF AVANT GARDE STUFF.

AFTER SEVERAL MONTHS, I HAD TRAINED MY EAR TO BE ABLE TO FOLLOW THE CONNECTION BETWEEN THE IMPROVISED SOLOS AND THEIR FOUNDATIONS, THE COMPOSITION'S CHORD STRUCTURE.

WOW! I THINK I HAVE IT DOWN. THE STRUCTURE OF THE IMPROVISING IS MUCH CLEARER NOW.

I STARTED BUYING AND COLLECTING JAZZ RECORDS, WHICH I'D TAKE TO MY BUDDY'S HOUSE, WHERE WE'D COMPARE NOTES ON THEM. I ALSO STARTED LEARNING ABOUT EARLIER FORMS OF JAZZ THAT I PREVIOUSLY HAD LITTLE INTEREST IN.

THIS STUFF BY COUNT BASIE'S EARLY BAND IS TREMENDOUS. NO WONDER THEY CALL IT SWING MUSIC--IT'S SO INFECTIOUS.

GOD, THAT LOUIS ARMSTRONG MATERIAL FROM THE 1920'S WAS JUST SEARING.

THESE EXPERIMENTAL TRACKS BY LENNIE TRISTANO ARE SUPPOSED TO BE "FREE" IMPROVISATIONS, NOT BASED ON ANY PRESET CHORD PROGRESSIONS. LET'S SEE WHAT THEY SOUND LIKE.

PRETTY SOON, I GOT MORE INVOLVED IN LEARNING ABOUT JAZZ, THE MUSIC ITSELF, NOT JUST ANECDOTES ABOUT THE MUSICIANS, THAN I'D EVER BEEN WITH ANY SUBJECT BEFORE--COMICS OR SPORTS MAGAZINES AND BOOKS INCLUDED.

YOU SAY YOUR FATHER'S SELLING HIS JAZZ 78'S FOR A DIME A PIECE? I'LL BE RIGHT OVER.

I ALSO SOUGHT THE KNOWLEDGE OF PEOPLE WHO'D BEEN CONNECTED WITH THE JAZZ SCENE FOR SOME TIME, MUSICIANS, DEE JAYS, COLLECTORS--I WAS FASCINATED.

WELL, LOOK, IS THERE ANY CHANCE WE CAN GET TOGETHER THIS WEEKEND? I'M WILLING TO BUY SOME OF YOUR RECORDS THAT YOU WANT TO GET RID OF.

I GOT A REAL LUCKY BREAK WHEN ONE OF MY FAVORITE JAZZ CRITICS, IRA GITLER IN NEW YORK, WAS WILLING TO CORRESPOND WITH ME. I LEARNED A LOT FROM HIM AND HE ALSO HELPED ME IN OTHER WAYS.

OH, MAN! ANOTHER LETTER FROM IRA GITLER. GREAT! THEY'RE SO SUBSTANTIVE.

SO, WHAT WAS I GONNA DO WITH ALL THIS STUFF I WAS LEARNING AND COLLECTING? WELL, RIGHT THERE IN HIGH SCHOOL, I WAS HAVING FUN WITH IT, BUT MY INTEREST WENT BEYOND THAT, AS WE'LL SEE.

THEN, IN MY SENIOR YEAR IN HIGH SCHOOL, I FINALLY LANDED A JOB I'D BEEN TRYING TO GET A HOLD OF FOR SOME TIME--AS AN USHER IN A NEIGHBORHOOD MOVIE THEATRE, ABOUT A BLOCK AWAY FROM MY HOUSE.

THE UNIFORMS ARE UPSTAIRS. JUST WEAR THE ONE THAT'S THE BEST MATCH.

NOW SHOWING
SOMEBODY UP THERE LIKES ME
STARRING PAUL NEWMAN

I WORKED EVENINGS AND WEEKENDS AND GOT TO MEET A LOT OF ADULTS THERE WHO I LIKED. JUST HAVING THAT OUTLET TOOK PRESSURE OFF ME. I DIDN'T TELL THEM ABOUT MY PROBLEMS, BUT LISTENING TO THEM TALK ABOUT THEIR OWN SITUATIONS GAVE ME PERSPECTIVE ON MINE.

ONE TIME, I WAS IN WHAT I THOUGHT AT THE TIME WAS A TERRIBLE SITUATION...

I ESPECIALLY LIKED COMING HOME AFTER WORK ON FRIDAY NIGHTS, THE BEGINNING OF SABBATH, WHEN EVERYONE ELSE AT HOME WAS ASLEEP.

THE HOUSE IS QUIET.

I'D GET SOME FOOD MADE FOR THE SABBATH OUT OF THE REFRIGERATOR, AND WATCH THE BOXING MATCHES, WHICH STARTED AT 10:00 PM, FOLLOWED BY A FIFTEEN-MINUTE SHOW CALLED "GREATEST FIGHTS OF THE CENTURY."

GREATEST FIGHTS

THERE I COULD SEE SOME OF THE GREATEST BOXERS OF THE PAST IN ACTION.

I REALLY FELT PEACEFUL AND RELAXED ON THESE FRIDAY NIGHTS AND LOOKED FORWARD TO THEM SO MUCH.

THESE SWEET INTERLUDES TOOK PLACE DURING MY LAST YEAR OF HIGH SCHOOL. I HAD NO WAY OF KNOWING WHAT I'D DO AFTER I GRADUATED.

I DIDN'T WANT TO GO TO COLLEGE, BECAUSE I THOUGHT WHEREVER I WENT I'D HAVE TO TAKE REQUIRED SCIENCE AND MATH COURSES THAT I'D FLUNK.

I HAD NO CONFIDENCE IN MY ABILITY IN MATH AND SCIENCE AND HAD ONCE QUIT A TENTH GRADE ALGEBRA COURSE RIGHT AFTER I'D SCREWED UP A TEST, BECAUSE I FELT I'D FAIL. THE REQUIRED "MATH" COURSE I WOUND UP TAKING WAS BOOKKEEPING.

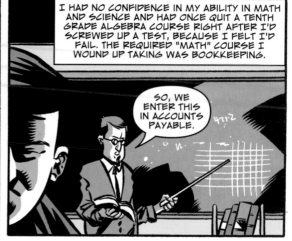

SO, WE ENTER THIS IN ACCOUNTS PAYABLE.

ONE THING I CONSIDERED DOING WAS JOINING THE NAVY, LIKE MY COUSIN, MORT, HAD DONE. AT LEAST IT WAS A SECURE JOB, ANYWAY.

IF I JOINED EVEN A DAY BEFORE MY EIGHTEENTH BIRTHDAY, I'D GET OUT BEFORE I WAS TWENTY-ONE. MAYBE I'D LEARN A TRADE IN THE NAVY, SO I COULD GET WORK WHEN I WAS DISCHARGED. OR MAYBE I'D MAKE IT A CAREER. AT LEAST THEY'D GIVE ME A PLACE TO STAY AND FEED ME.

I ALSO LEARNED ABOUT BEING ABLE TO GET U.S. FILE CLERK JOBS BY TAKING CIVIL SERVICE TESTS. SO, I TOOK ONE AND PASSED IT AND THEN WAITED TO SEE IF THEY'D CALL ME.

AFTER I GRADUATED, THE FIRST JOB I GOT WAS IN MY UNCLE'S AUTOMOBILE JUNK YARD AND CAR PARTS STORE. I MADE FIFTY BUCKS A WEEK WORKING FORTY-EIGHT HOURS.

I DIDN'T LIKE THE WORK, WHICH WAS DIRTY AND BORING. AND, AGAIN, IT WAS WITH RELATIVES.

AFTER A COUPLE OF WEEKS THOUGH, I GOT AN OFFER FROM THE U.S. RAILROAD RETIREMENT BOARD OF A THREE-MONTH APPOINTMENT AS FILE CLERK.

I PROBABLY SHOULD'VE TAKEN THE JOB A LOT MORE SERIOUSLY THAN I DID. I GOOFED ON IT, BECAUSE IT WAS TEMPORARY, THE WORK WAS UNINTERESTING, AND THE PAY WAS BAD.

I DID THE WORK, BUT THAT TOOK ME NO TIME, AND AFTER I WAS DONE, I'D SCREW AROUND WITH THE OTHER FILE CLERKS, WHO WERE ALSO TEMPS.

HEY, MAN, GIMME SOME OF YOUR SANDWICH. IT LOOKS GOOD.

NATURALLY, THAT DIDN'T MAKE THE BOSSES VERY HAPPY WITH US.

YOU GUYS SHOULDN'T HAVE ANY PROBLEM WITH THIS WORK. IT'S JUST MANUAL LABOR, THAT'S ALL.

MY GOD, YOU ACT LIKE IT WAS ROCKET SCIENCE.

LITTLE DID I KNOW, HOWEVER, THAT I WOULD SPEND THE REST OF MY LIFE DOING WORK LIKE THIS AND EVENTUALLY LEARN TO TOLERATE IT.

ACTUALLY, MAYBE I SHOULDA STAYED WITH THE CIVIL SERVICE, WHICH I EVENTUALLY GOT BACK INTO ANYWAY.

IT WAS CLEAN, EASY WORK; IT HAD FRINGE BENEFITS; AND, AS I DIDN'T REALIZE, BECAUSE I WAS LIVING WITH MY PARENTS AT THE TIME, I COULD'VE SUPPORTED MYSELF IN MY OWN APARTMENT ON THE MONEY I MADE.

OF COURSE, WHAT HAPPENED TO ME IN THE YEARS DURING THE LATE 1950'S AND EARLY 60'S, WHEN I DIDN'T WORK FOR THE FEDERAL GOVERNMENT, WAS VERY IMPORTANT.

I DON'T KNOW HOW MUCH WOULDN'T HAVE HAPPENED IF I'D JUST STAYED WITH THE GOVERNMENT RIGHT THROUGH.

OH WELL, IT'S PROBABLY IDLE SPECULATION. IN THE LONG RUN, WE'RE ALL DEAD ANYWAY.

IN ANY EVENT, WHEN MY APPOINTMENT WITH THE RAILROAD RETIREMENT BOARD WAS UP, IT WAS ALMOST TIME FOR MY EIGHTEENTH BIRTHDAY, SO I FIGURED...

THE ONLY THING LEFT FOR ME IS THE NAVY.

I DID THIS WITH A CERTAIN AMOUNT OF TREPIDATION. I AM REALLY CLUMSY WITH MECHANICAL STUFF, AND I KNEW YOU HAD TO DO A CERTAIN AMOUNT OF THAT IN THE BASIC TRAINING OF ANY BRANCH OF THE SERVICE. COULD I GET THROUGH IT?

I WONDER IF THEY EXPECT ME TO DO HEAVY-DUTY MECHANICAL STUFF?

THE TRAIN CAME AND PICKED US UP, AND IT TOOK ABOUT EIGHTEEN HOURS TO GET FROM CLEVELAND TO GREAT LAKES NAVAL BASE, OUTSIDE CHICAGO.

♪ WHATTYA TOOOOT! MAMA? ♪

IN THAT TIME, THEY MUST'VE PLAYED THE EVERLY BROTHERS' "WAKE UP LITTLE SUSIE" FIVE-HUNDRED TIMES.

SO, WE'RE GETTING PROCESSED AND CHECKED IN AND DOING WHAT WE'RE SUPPOSED TO BE DOING TO BECOME MEMBERS OF THE NAVY, AND EVERYBODY'S GETTING YELLED AT, BUT THAT'S WHAT'S SUPPOSED TO BE HAPPENING, SO I FEEL O.K.

THEY MADE ME EDUCATION CHIEF OF MY GROUP BECAUSE I GOT A HIGH TEST SCORE.

EVERYTHING'S GOING O.K. FOR ABOUT A WEEK AND THEN, ONE DAY, THEY GIVE US ALL THESE CLOTHES AND EQUIPMENT AND STUFF, AND THEY TELL US HOW TO PACK THEM IN OUR BAGS OR LOCKER OR BOTH AND HOW TO TAKE CARE OF THEM.

YOU TAKE THESE SOCKS AND THEN YOU...

MAN, FROM THE MINUTE THAT GUY STARTED TALKING, MY MIND WENT BLANK. I COULDN'T HEAR HIM. IT WAS LIKE WHEN TEACHERS TOLD ME ABOUT MATH OR SCIENCE OR AUTOMOBILES, ONLY WORSE.

I DIDN'T TAKE A THING IN, NOTHING. THE OTHER GUYS SEEMED LIKE THEY WERE GETTING AT LEAST A LITTLE OF IT, BUT ME, NOTHING.

I THINK ABOUT THAT MOMENT, AND I THINK ABOUT MY MOTHER AND HOW SHE WOULDN'T ALLOW ME TO OWN A BICYCLE BECAUSE SHE SAID I WAS TOO IRRESPONSIBLE. I GUESS SHE WAS RIGHT.

I DON'T KNOW WHAT'S CAUSING IT, BUT, TO THIS DAY, I'M NO GOOD AT TECHNICAL STUFF. I GO TO A CLASS ON HOW TO USE A COMPUTER AND PEOPLE OLDER THAN ME GET IT AND I DON'T.

I WAS HAVING SOME DOUBTS ABOUT WHETHER I'D GET THROUGH NAVY BASIC TRAINING OR NOT. MAN, I FELT SICK.

THEN WE WERE ORDERED TO WASH OUR CLOTHES AND GET OUR STUFF READY FOR AN INSPECTION. MAN, I WAS TOTALLY SHOCKED. I DIDN'T KNOW ANYTHING ABOUT DOING HAND LAUNDRY.

NEITHER DID A BUNCH OF OTHER GUYS WHO WERE IN MY UNIT, I BET, BUT THEY COULD FIGURE OUT WHAT TO DO AND I COULDN'T.

EVERYONE FINISHED THEIR LAUNDRY BUT ME. I COULDN'T FIGURE WHICH CLOTHES WERE CLEAN AND WHICH WERE DIRTY. I DIDN'T KNOW IF THE OTHERS HAD DONE A BETTER JOB THAN ME OR NOT. BUT WHEN THEY CAME TO STOP US, I WAS THE ONLY ONE LEFT WASHING AT THE SINK. I HAD CRACKED UP, WAS IN A STATE OF SHOCK.

THE GUYS WERE YELLING AT ME TO COME AWAY FROM THE SINK, BUT I COULDN'T BECAUSE MY CLOTHES WEREN'T DONE.

C'MON, HARVEY, FINISH UP.

I FINALLY RELENTED AND WENT TO BED WITH MY WASHING WET AND ALL BALLED UP.

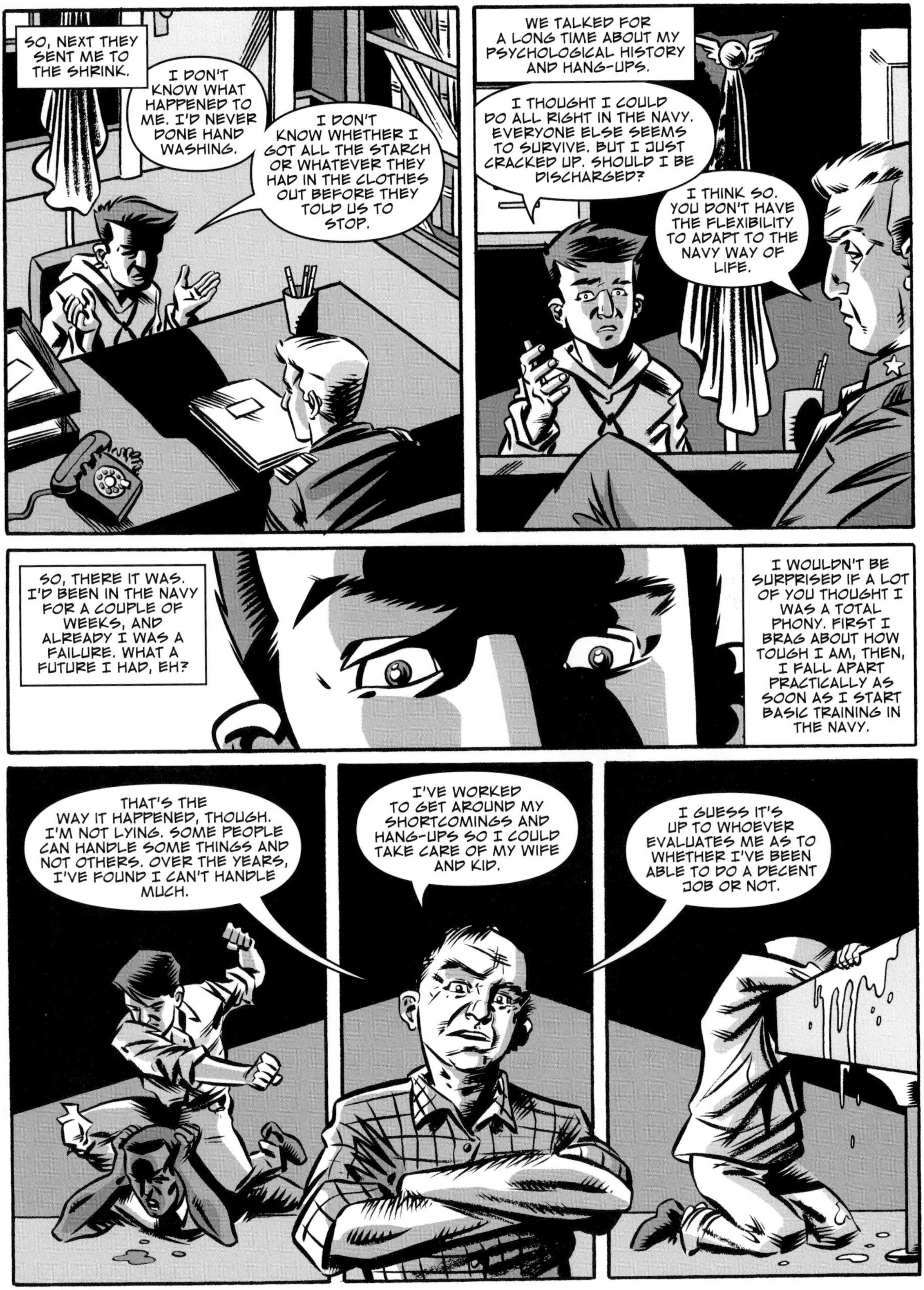
SO, NEXT THEY SENT ME TO THE SHRINK.
I DON'T KNOW WHAT HAPPENED TO ME. I'D NEVER DONE HAND WASHING.
I DON'T KNOW WHETHER I GOT ALL THE STARCH OR WHATEVER THEY HAD IN THE CLOTHES OUT BEFORE THEY TOLD US TO STOP.
WE TALKED FOR A LONG TIME ABOUT MY PSYCHOLOGICAL HISTORY AND HANG-UPS.
I THOUGHT I COULD DO ALL RIGHT IN THE NAVY. EVERYONE ELSE SEEMS TO SURVIVE. BUT I JUST CRACKED UP. SHOULD I BE DISCHARGED?
I THINK SO. YOU DON'T HAVE THE FLEXIBILITY TO ADAPT TO THE NAVY WAY OF LIFE.
SO, THERE IT WAS. I'D BEEN IN THE NAVY FOR A COUPLE OF WEEKS, AND ALREADY I WAS A FAILURE. WHAT A FUTURE I HAD, EH?
I WOULDN'T BE SURPRISED IF A LOT OF YOU THOUGHT I WAS A TOTAL PHONY. FIRST I BRAG ABOUT HOW TOUGH I AM, THEN, I FALL APART PRACTICALLY AS SOON AS I START BASIC TRAINING IN THE NAVY.
THAT'S THE WAY IT HAPPENED, THOUGH. I'M NOT LYING. SOME PEOPLE CAN HANDLE SOME THINGS AND NOT OTHERS. OVER THE YEARS, I'VE FOUND I CAN'T HANDLE MUCH.
I'VE WORKED TO GET AROUND MY SHORTCOMINGS AND HANG-UPS SO I COULD TAKE CARE OF MY WIFE AND KID.
I GUESS IT'S UP TO WHOEVER EVALUATES ME AS TO WHETHER I'VE BEEN ABLE TO DO A DECENT JOB OR NOT.

SO, ANYWAY, AFTER THEY DETERMINED THEY WERE GOING TO DISCHARGE ME, THEY PUT ME IN THIS UNIT WITH OTHER GUYS THAT WERE BEING DISCHARGED. SOME OF THEM WERE REALLY MESSED UP--ALL THE WAY FROM CATATONIC TO HYPER.

I LOOKED AT THEM AND I THOUGHT, "I BELONG WITH THESE GUYS NOW." I GOT MORE THAN AN INKLING THAT I WASN'T GOING TO HAVE AN EASY TIME GETTING THROUGH THE REST OF MY LIFE.

THEY HELD ME IN THIS UNIT ABOUT A WEEK OR TEN DAYS, THEN SENT ME HOME WEARING THESE SALVATION ARMY TYPE CLOTHES. (THE STUFF I'D WORN GOING INTO BASIC TRAINING HAD ALREADY BEEN SHIPPED HOME.)

I TOOK THE TRAIN BACK AND I WAS FEELING REALLY HELPLESS AND DISCOURAGED ON THE RIDE. WHAT COULD I DO WITH MYSELF?

I GRADUATE FROM HIGH SCHOOL AND A YEAR LATER, I FIND I'M NOT FIT TO DO ANYTHING.

I CAN'T REMEMBER WHAT MY MOTHER SAID WHEN I GOT BACK HOME. I CAN IMAGINE WHAT SHE THOUGHT WHEN I CAME BACK SO SOON-- PROBABLY SOMETHING ABOUT MY BEING IRRESPONSIBLE AND SPOILED. I GIVE HER CREDIT FOR ONE THING, SHE KNEW I HAD PSYCHOLOGICAL PROBLEMS BEFORE A WHOLE LOT OF OTHER PEOPLE.

WELL, WHAT COULD I DO? I HAD TO GET A JOB AGAIN. I WENT BACK TO THE RAILROAD RETIREMENT BOARD TO SEE IF I COULD GET ANOTHER TEMPORARY APPOINTMENT.

THEY TOOK ME BACK FOR A ONE-MONTH APPOINTMENT. THE BOSS SAID--

PEKAR, THE LAST TIME YOU WERE HERE, YOU WERE OBNOXIOUS. I HOPE YOU LEARNED SOMETHING BY YOUR EXPERIENCES IN THE NAVY. IF YOU CONDUCT YOURSELF PROPERLY THIS TIME, WE MAY HAVE A PERMANENT POSITION FOR YOU.

A PERMANENT POSITION. YEAH, MAYBE I OUGHTA SHOOT FOR THAT. MAYBE I CAN GET BY WITH THAT. IF I WORK HERE FOR A WHILE, I'LL MAYBE GET RAISES. IT'S NOT GOING TO TAKE MUCH TO SUPPORT ME. I'LL NEVER GET MARRIED. I DON'T EVEN DATE NOW.

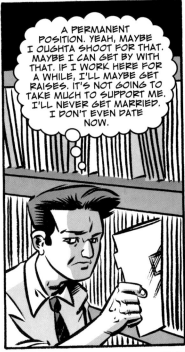

BUT INCORRIGIBLE SCREW-UP THAT I AM, I STARTED GOOFING ON THE GIG FROM PRACTICALLY DAY ONE. WHEN MY APPOINTMENT WAS OVER, I WASN'T OFFERED A THING.

GOD, I BLEW A CHANCE TO GET A FULL-TIME JOB, AS HARD AS THEY ARE TO FIND THESE DAYS. AM I A TOTAL WASTE?

IT TURNED OUT THOUGH, THAT THERE WERE SEVERAL FEDERAL AGENCIES THAT HAD FILE CLERK JOBS. I GOT ANOTHER ONE IN CLEVELAND AT THE NAVY FINANCE CENTER, AS A CIVILIAN EMPLOYEE.

FOR SOME REASON, I DID WELL AT THE NAVY FINANCE CENTER. THE PEOPLE THERE WERE OLDER, SO I DIDN'T HAVE AS MUCH INCLINATION TO SCREW AROUND AS I DID BEFORE.

ALSO, I LIKED TALKING TO THE ADULTS ABOUT STUFF. THEY WERE DOWN-TO-EARTH PEOPLE AND IT SEEMED I COULD ALMOST ALWAYS FIND SOME PLEASANT, IF NOT EARTH-SHAKING, TOPIC TO DISCUSS.

SO, WHEN DID YOU GRADUATE FROM JOHN ADAMS? BECAUSE I HAD A LOTTA COUSINS THAT WENT THERE. YOU COULDA KNOWN ONE.

WHILE I WAS AT THE NAVY FINANCE CENTER, I TOOK A CIVIL SERVICE EXAM FOR THE POST OFFICE. THAT WAS MY DREAM JOB, I THOUGHT. A CARRIER JOB PAID WAY BETTER THAN THE FILE CLERK GIGS I HAD BEEN GETTING.

PLUS, YOU WERE ON YOUR OWN, DELIVERING THE MAIL. NOBODY WAS OUT THERE SUPERVISING YOU.

SO, I WAS WAITING TO SEE IF I HAD PASSED THE TEST FOR MONTHS.

I FINALLY FOUND OUT THAT I'D PASSED IT, BUT I HAD TO WAIT AROUND SOME MORE FOR AN OPENING TO OCCUR AND FOR ME TO GET ASSIGNED THERE.

WELL, AT LEAST I PASSED.

FINALLY, I WAS TOLD I HAD A JOB IN EAST CLEVELAND, AT THIS TIME AN OLD BUT PRETTY PROSPEROUS INNER RING SUBURB OF CLEVELAND.

IT WAS WITH MIXED FEELINGS THAT I LEFT THE NAVY FINANCE CENTER TO WORK AT THE POST OFFICE. I'D REALLY DEVELOPED SOME PLEASANT RELATIONS THERE. AT THAT TIME, I DIDN'T REALIZE HOW IMPORTANT IT WAS TO BE COMFORTABLE ON A JOB.

BYE, I'LL MISS EVERYONE.

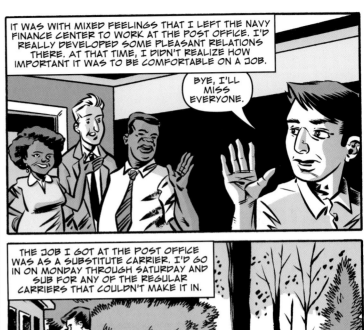

THE JOB I GOT AT THE POST OFFICE WAS AS A SUBSTITUTE CARRIER. I'D GO IN ON MONDAY THROUGH SATURDAY AND SUB FOR ANY OF THE REGULAR CARRIERS THAT COULDN'T MAKE IT IN.

EAST CLEVELAND WAS PRETTY FAR FROM WHERE I LIVED AND PUBLIC TRANSPORTATION OUT THERE WASN'T TOO HOT AROUND 6:00 AM, WHEN I WAS SUPPOSED TO COME IN. SO, HAVING RECENTLY GOTTEN MY DRIVER'S LICENSE, I BOUGHT A CAR.

WOW! I NEVER THOUGHT I'D GET A DRIVER'S LICENSE.

I WENT OUT WITH MY SUPPOSEDLY EXPERT COUSIN TO A USED CAR LOT AND PICKED UP A 1950 CHEVY WITH A NEW PAINT JOB FOR $325.00.

THE PAINT JOB WAS THE BEST THING ABOUT THE CAR. I HAD IT FOR A COUPLE OF YEARS AND IT DROVE ME NUTS. IT WAS ALWAYS BREAKING DOWN, I.E. NOT STARTING, BUT NOBODY IN THE MANY GAS STATIONS I TOOK IT TO COULD FIGURE OUT WHAT THE BASIC PROBLEM WAS. THEY'D GET IT STARTED, BUT A FEW WEEKS OR MONTHS LATER, IT'D CONK OUT AGAIN.

SO, I GO TO THE EAST CLEVELAND P.O. BRIGHT AND EARLY ON A MONDAY AND THEY HOOK ME UP WITH A CARRIER I WAS SUPPOSED TO GO AROUND WITH AND WATCH.

THE GUY SHOWED ME HOW TO BREAK DOWN THE MAIL IN A CASE, TIE IT INTO BUNDLES AND SEND IT OUT TO DIFFERENT BOXES ON THE ROUTE WHERE SOME WOULD BE STORED TO PICK UP AND DELIVER.

AFTER THAT, WE'D GO OUT AND DELIVER STUFF. WE GOT THROUGH A COUPLE OF HOURS EARLY, BUT NOBODY TOLD ME I SHOULD HANG AROUND UNTIL IT WAS TIME TO GO AND THEN CLOCK OUT. LIKE A DUMMY, I COULDN'T FIGURE THAT OUT FOR MYSELF.

NO, WHAT I DID WAS TO CLOCK OUT EARLY WHATEVER TIME I FINISHED--1:00, 1:30, THUS DEPRIVING MYSELF OF TWO OR TWO AND A HALF HOURS' PAY.

SO, THEN I STARTED THINKING THAT I WASN'T BEING HIRED TO WORK AND BE PAID FOR AN EIGHT-HOUR DAY, ONLY JUST AS LONG AS IT TOOK TO DELIVER THE DAY'S MAIL.

RING

AND THEN I STARTED WORRYING ABOUT WHETHER I COULD CONSISTENTLY TIE THE BUNDLES OF MAIL TIGHT ENOUGH SO THAT THEY WOULDN'T FALL APART EN ROUTE TO THE BOXES.

ALL THE REST OF THE WEEK, I OBSESSED ABOUT HAVING BUNDLES OF MAIL BREAKING EVERY TIME I WENT TO DELIVER MAIL AND ABOUT NOT WORKING AN EIGHT-HOUR DAY.

WHAT IF THIS? WHAT IF THAT?

BY FRIDAY, I WAS SO SHOOK UP, I COULDN'T GET OUT OF BED. THAT'S THE ONLY TIME BEFORE OR SINCE THAT I WAS UNABLE TO GO TO WORK BECAUSE I WAS TOO NERVOUS.

I THOUGHT I HAD RUN OUT OF OPTIONS, THAT THIS WAS PRETTY MUCH THE END OF THE LINE FOR ME. SO, I WAS THINKING ABOUT WHAT I COULD DO TO KEEP GOING, AND SUDDENLY, COLLEGE DIDN'T SEEM TO BE A BAD IDEA FOR ME.

MAYBE I COULD MAKE IT THROUGH COLLEGE, MAYBE I COULD FIND A WAY TO GET AROUND THOSE COMPULSORY MATH COURSES. I ANNOUNCED TO MY LONG-SUFFERING MOTHER THAT I WAS SERIOUSLY CONSIDERING GOING TO COLLEGE. I THINK SHE WAS PLEASED ABOUT THAT. WHERE ELSE SHOULD AN EIGHTEEN-YEAR-OLD JEWISH BOY BE?

I GUESS I'LL TRY COLLEGE.

IT WAS LATE IN MAY, BUT I WAS ABLE TO GET INTO THIS LOCAL UNIVERSITY, WESTERN RESERVE, IN TIME FOR THE SUMMER SEMESTER COURSES, ALL EASY SUBJECTS FOR ME.

IF YOU'D JUST FILL OUT THESE FORMS, MR. PEKAR.

MAN, IT STARTED OUT SO EASILY FOR ME. I HAD REMEMBERED ALL THE STUFF I LEARNED IN MY HIGH SCHOOL HISTORY AND GEOGRAPHY, AND THAT'S WHAT I STARTED OUT TAKING IN COLLEGE--BEGINNING HISTORY AND GEOGRAPHY.

THE HIGH SCHOOL MATERIAL WAS OFTEN REPEATED IN THE COLLEGE COURSES. I HAD ABSOLUTELY NO TROUBLE WITH THEM.

IN FACT, SOME OF THE OTHER STUDENTS MIGHT'VE BEEN AMAZED BY HOW I, A FIRST YEAR STUDENT, WAS PREPARED FOR THEM. ACTUALLY, IT WAS NOTHING BUT MY TRICK MEMORY.

MAN, YOU SEEM TO KNOW THE ANSWERS BEFORE THE TEACHER ASKS THE QUESTION.

THAT SUMMER WAS A REAL HAPPY TIME FOR ME. I WAS ACTUALLY GETTING RESPECT FOR THE 3.75 AVERAGE I AMASSED, PLUS THE WEATHER WAS FINE.

I STILL HAD MY CAR AND ACTUALLY HAD A FEW DATES. NO SERIOUS RELATIONSHIPS RESULTED, BUT AT LEAST I WAS IN THE BALL GAME. THERE'D BEEN A TIME WHEN I NEVER THOUGHT I'D BE ABLE TO FIND A WOMAN WHO WANTED TO GO OUT WITH ME.

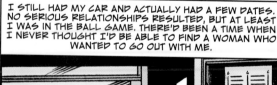

IT SEEMS STRANGE, LOOKING BACK ON IT, HOW OPTIMISTIC I FELT AT THE TIME. I THOUGHT I'D FINALLY MADE A CORRECT MOVE IN GOING TO COLLEGE.

WHO'D A THOUGHT COLLEGE WOULD WORK OUT SO WELL? MAYBE I'M ON THE RIGHT TRACK NOW.

IN THE SUMMER, I'D TAKEN COURSES WITH A LOT OF OLDER PEOPLE, LIKE SCHOOL TEACHERS, BUT WHEN FALL SEMESTER CAME, I WAS IN WITH STUDENTS MY OWN AGE.

A FEW I KNEW FROM HIGH SCHOOL, AND THEY HOOKED ME UP WITH OTHER WRU STUDENTS. NOW I HAD A NEW SET OF FRIENDS.

THIS WAS MORE OF AN INTELLECTUAL SCENE. SOME OF THESE PEOPLE WERE FOLLOWERS OF THE BEATNIK MOVEMENT. EVERYONE SEEMED TO BE WRITING POETRY.

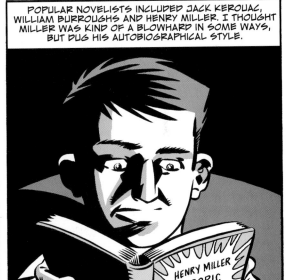

POPULAR NOVELISTS INCLUDED JACK KEROUAC, WILLIAM BURROUGHS AND HENRY MILLER. I THOUGHT MILLER WAS KIND OF A BLOWHARD IN SOME WAYS, BUT DUG HIS AUTOBIOGRAPHICAL STYLE.

HENRY MILLER
TROPIC OF CANCER

I WAS STILL HEAVILY INTO JAZZ, STILL TRYING TO LEARN AS MUCH AS I COULD ABOUT IT, AND WAS REGARDED AS A LOCAL EXPERT BY SOME OF THE PEOPLE I WENT TO SCHOOL WITH.

CHECK OUT THIS MILES DAVIS COLUMBIA RECORD.

HE'S GOT THIS EXTREMELY ORIGINAL TENOR SAX PLAYER ON IT, JOHN COLTRANE, AND ONE OF THE BEST RHYTHM SECTIONS IN JAZZ.

I STILL KEPT UP MY CORRESPONDENCE WITH IRA GITLER, WHO HIPPED ME TO THE PROMISING NEW YOUNG MUSICIANS IN NEW YORK BEFORE THEY BECAME NATIONALLY KNOWN.

LETTERS FROM IRA ARE LIKE GOLD!

AND I STILL WOULD MEET UP WITH MY TRUMPET-PLAYING FRIEND, WHO WAS NOW GOING TO THE MANHATTAN SCHOOL OF MUSIC IN NEW YORK BUT WOULD COME HOME ON VACATIONS AND IN THE SUMMER.

WHAT DO YOU THINK ABOUT THIS NEW THIRD STREAM MOVEMENT, WHERE THEY'RE BLENDING AVANT GARDE JAZZ AND MODERN CLASSICAL MUSIC?

AND, HEY, MODERN CLASSICAL STUFF WAS CONSIDERED HIP--STRAVINSKY, BARTOK, SCHOENBERG, BERG, WEBER, IT HAD A FOLLOWING IN THE BEATNIK ERA.

AND THE CONCERT WILL CONCLUDE WITH ALBAN BERG'S TWENTIETH CENTURY OPERA "LULU."

THEN THERE WAS A LOT OF INTEREST IN FOLK MUSIC, LIKE PETE SEEGER AND WOODY GUTHRIE. BEATNIKS AND THEIR FOLLOWERS WERE INTO AN ADMIRABLY BROAD SPECTRUM OF MUSIC.

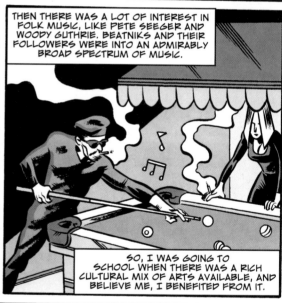

SO, I WAS GOING TO SCHOOL WHEN THERE WAS A RICH CULTURAL MIX OF ARTS AVAILABLE, AND BELIEVE ME, I BENEFITED FROM IT.

FOR A WHILE, I EVEN TOOK UP PLAYING TRUMPET, BUT I COULDN'T GET ENOUGH TIME TO PRACTICE, SO I LET IT GO, LIKE I HAVE SO MANY OTHER POTENTIALLY CONSTRUCTIVE PURSUITS.

ANYWAY, THE NEXT TWO SEMESTERS I TOOK UP ENGLISH, AND HAD A REAL FINE TEACHER IN MS. WATERMAN.

SHE WAS AN OLDER WOMAN FROM BOSTON WITH A SHARP SENSE OF HUMOR. I SAW RIGHT AWAY WHERE MY WRITING WAS PRETENTIOUS AND SLOPPILY CONSTRUCTED, AND, WITH HER HELP, WAS ABLE TO IMPROVE AND STREAMLINE IT QUITE A BIT.

THIS PAPER IS QUITE AN IMPROVEMENT.

B+

AFTER I HAD FINISHED UP TWO MORE SEMESTERS AT WRU, I DECIDED I WOULD HITCHHIKE TO NEW YORK THE FOLLOWING SUMMER. I HAD COUSINS THERE AND THOUGHT I COULD CRASH WITH THEM AND SEE IF I COULD GET A JOB IN THE APPLE.

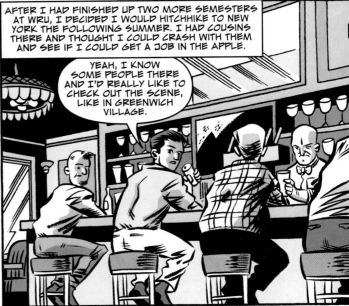

YEAH, I KNOW SOME PEOPLE THERE AND I'D REALLY LIKE TO CHECK OUT THE SCENE, LIKE IN GREENWICH VILLAGE.

IT WAS WEIRD FOR ME TO DO SOMETHING LIKE THAT. USUALLY, I WAS AFRAID OF EVERYTHING. I'M SURPRISED MY MOTHER TOOK IT AS CALMLY AS SHE DID.

WELL, I HOPE YOU'LL BE CAREFUL AND REMEMBER TO CONTACT YOUR RELATIVES WHILE YOU ARE IN NEW YORK.

SO I TOOK OFF ONE DAY, AND IT TOOK ME ABOUT TWELVE HOURS TO GET TO NEW YORK CITY.

WHEN I GOT IN, IT WAS ABOUT FOUR IN THE MORNING. I DIDN'T KNOW WHAT TO DO. I CALLED MY COUSIN, WHO WAS MARRIED TO THIS GUY WHO WAS A RABBI IN BROOKLYN.

YEAH, I'M OVER HERE IN LOWER MANHATTAN, I THINK.

PHONE BOO

THEY GAVE ME INSTRUCTIONS ON HOW I COULD TAKE THE SUBWAY INTO BROOKLYN, THE FLATBUSH SECTION, SO I WAS GETTING PULLED RIGHT INTO THE SCENE.

I FOUND THEIR APARTMENT, AND I RANG THE BELL. THEY WERE WAITING FOR ME. I GOTTA ADMIT THEY TREATED ME VERY WELL, TOO.

HI.

YEARS LATER, WE GOT INTO A HUGE HASSLE WHEN I SENT A LETTER TO MY LOCAL NEWSPAPER CRITICAL OF ISRAEL INVADING LEBANON, AND I'VE NEVER SPOKEN TO THEM AGAIN. HOWEVER, WE DIDN'T GET INTO ANY FOREIGN POLICY DISCUSSIONS WHILE I WAS THERE IN 1959.

SO, HOW'S Y'BRUTHUH, HAWRIE? HE DOIN' O.K.?

ANYWAY, THE RABBI REALLY TRIED HARD TO GET A JOB FOR ME. HE TOOK ME INTO PLACE AFTER PLACE LOOKING.

SIR, I HAVE A YOUNG MAN WHO IS IN MY CHARGE THAT I'M SEEKING WORK FOR.

YES.

FINALLY, HE GOT ME A GIG AT THE CAFE BIZARRE, IN GREENWICH VILLAGE, THIS RIP-OFF TOURIST TRAP WHERE PEOPLE WOULD COME IN LOOKING FOR THE AUTHENTIC BEATNIKS.

A FEW BONA FIDE POETS DID SHOW UP TO READ THEIR STUFF FOR TIPS, BUT THE WHOLE SCENE WAS PRETTY SAD, MOSTLY TOURISTS LOOKING AT OTHER TOURISTS.

YOUR ORDER, SIR?

I WASN'T MAKING ANY KIND OF BREAD TO SPEAK OF THERE, SO, AFTER A WHILE, I DECIDED TO SPLIT. THE WAITERS GIGS WERE THE ONLY KIND THAT WERE OPEN.

Cafe BIZARRE

BEFORE I LEFT NEW YORK CITY, I GOT TO SEE IRA GITLER. HE WAS REALLY NICE TO ME.

HERE'S SOMETHING THAT I THINK YOU'LL DIG HEARING--DIZZY WITH CAB CALLOWAY.

IRA LIVED IN THIS BIG APARTMENT ON WEST END AVENUE, THAT WAS RENT-CONTROLLED, WITH HIS FAMILY. WHAT A GREAT DEAL THEY HAD!

HEY, I WANTED TO TELL YOU ABOUT THIS NEW MAGAZINE, *THE JAZZ REVIEW.*

YEAH, I'VE BOUGHT ALL THE ISSUES SO FAR. IT'S GREAT.

WELL, THEY'RE LOOKING FOR WRITERS. I THINK YOU OUGHT TO SUBMIT SOMETHING TO THEM.

AW, IRA, THAT'S A REAL TOP-QUALITY MAGAZINE. YOU THINK THEY'D CONSIDER SOMETHING BY ME? I'VE NEVER BEEN PUBLISHED.

I DON'T KNOW IF THE COMPETITION'S GONNA BE AS TOUGH AS YOU THINK. THEY DON'T PAY ANYTHING, SO A LOT OF WRITERS AREN'T INTERESTED IN GOING WITH THEM.

STILL, IT'S SUCH A HIGH-CLASS MAGAZINE...

BUT YOU HAVEN'T GIVEN ME A BUM STEER YET. I GUESS IT WOULDN'T HURT TO TRY.

ACTUALLY, I'VE BEEN THINKING ABOUT WRITING SOMETHING FOR THEM ABOUT FATS NAVARRO. A COUPLE OF THEIR WRITERS HAVE INDICATED THAT HE WAS JUST A COPY OF DIZZY, BUT HE WAS WAY MORE ORIGINAL THAN THAT. HOW COULD HE HAVE INFLUENCED CLIFFORD BROWN SO MUCH IF HE WASN'T ORIGINAL?

ALSO, I'D LIKE TO DO SOMETHING ON THAD JONES. THERE'S NOBODY OUT THERE WITH A STYLE CLOSE TO HIS.

WELL, THERE Y'GO. YOU KNOW WHAT YOU'RE TALKING ABOUT, AND YOUR WRITING IN THE LETTERS YOU'VE SENT ME IS FINE. TAKE A SHOT AT IT.

YEAH, WHEN I GET BACK, MAYBE I WILL.

AFTER I GOT BACK TO CLEVELAND, I FOUND A GIG AS A COUNTER MAN IN A DELICATESSEN IN THE SUBURBS. I THINK I GOT IT THROUGH THE JEWISH VOCATIONAL SERVICE.

I GO DOWN THERE AND IT'S ANOTHER ONE OF THESE $1.00 AN HOUR, FIFTY HOURS A WEEK GIGS, WHERE THEY EXPECT YOU TO WORK YOUR ASS OFF LIKE YOU OWN THE PLACE.

AND DON'T GIVE THE CUSTOMERS ANY MORE THAN A 1/4 POUND CORNED BEEF SANDWICH, INCLUDING THE BREAD.

THAT JOB DIDN'T LAST TOO LONG. THEY HIRED ME AS SUMMER EMPLOYMENT, BUT THEY DECIDED THEY WANTED SOMEONE FULL TIME, SO I WAS LET GO AFTER TWO WEEKS.

I GOT A JOB RIGHT AFTER THAT AS A PLAYGROUND SUPERVISOR AT ONE OF THE CLEVELAND ELEMENTARY SCHOOLS.

THE FIRST DAY I REPORTED TO THAT GIG, IT WAS RAINING VERY HEAVILY. I FIGURED WE'D BE COOPED UP INDOORS FOR AT LEAST PART OF THE TIME, SO I BROUGHT THE MATERIAL I WAS GOING TO BASE A LETTER-TO-THE-EDITOR OF *JAZZ REVIEW* ON FATS NAVARRO.

HI, I'M HARVEY PEKAR. I'M SUPPOSED TO START WORKING TODAY, ALTHOUGH WITH THIS RAIN, THERE ISN'T TOO MUCH WE CAN DO RIGHT NOW.

HI, I'M LEN GOLDSTEIN. I ACTUALLY TEACH AT THIS SCHOOL DURING THE YEAR. THIS IS KATHERINE AND JUSTINE. THEY GO TO JOHN CARROLL AND OHIO UNIVERSITIES.

NICE TO MEET YOU.

HI.

HELLO.

SAY, LEN, I WAS WORKING ON THIS LETTER-TO-THE-EDITOR THAT I MIGHT TURN INTO AN ARTICLE FOR A JAZZ MAGAZINE. AS LONG AS IT'S RAINING AND WE'RE ALL SITTING AROUND IN THIS ROOM, D'YOU THINK I CAN KEEP ON WORKING ON IT UNTIL THE RAIN LETS UP AND WE GO OUTSIDE?

SURE, MIGHT AS WELL DO SOMETHING. IT BEATS SITTING ON YOUR HANDS.

2:00.

3:00.

WOW, LEN, THE RAIN DOESN'T LOOK LIKE IT'S GONNA LET UP SOON.

YEAH, IT'S STILL COMING DOWN HARD.

WELL, LOOK, I WANTED T' ASK YOU IF YOU'D BE WILLING T' LOOK AT THIS THING I'M WRITING. I JUST WANT TO KNOW IF WHAT I'M SAYING SEEMS REASONABLE. I THINK IT IS, BUT I'D LIKE SOMEONE ELSE'S OPINION.

OKAY, BRING IT OVER.

HERE IT IS.

UH, HEY, LEN, DID YOU READ THAT THING YET?

YEAH, HARVEY. IT'S FINE, VERY CLEAR AND UNDER-STANDABLE.

OF COURSE, I DON'T KNOW IF YOUR IDEAS ARE ANY GOOD. I DON'T KNOW ANYTHING ABOUT JAZZ.

"WELL, WHAT I SAY MIGHT BE CONTROVERSIAL, I DUNNO. THE GUY I'M WRITIN' ABOUT HASN'T GOTTEN THE CREDIT HE DESERVES YET.

"STILL, THE FACT THAT YOU FOUND IT CLEAR IS GOOD. AT LEAST PEOPLE WILL KNOW WHERE I STAND.

"I'VE SORT OF BEEN THINKING I'D LIKE TO BE A JAZZ CRITIC LATELY, AND THIS IS MY FIRST STEP IN THAT DIRECTION."

FINE. UH, LISTEN, HARVEY, DID THEY TELL YOU TO SHOW UP DOWNTOWN FOR OUR MEETING TOMORROW?

YEAH, I'VE GOT EVERYTHING WRITTEN DOWN.

GOOD... HEY, LOOK, THE SUN'S COME OUT AND THERE ARE SOME KIDS ON THE PLAYGROUND. LET'S GET OUT THERE.

THE DAY IS PRETTY UNEVENTFUL. THE KIDS GET ALONG FINE, THERE ARE NO FIGHTS TO BREAK UP.

AT THE END OF THE DAY...

WELL, SEE YOU GUYS IN THE MORNING.

YUP, TAKE IT EASY.

I PARK MY CAR DOWNTOWN THE NEXT DAY AND GO INSIDE THE MEETING.

THE BOSS OF THE SUMMER PROGRAM IS LECTURING.

AND WE WANT YOU TO BE USING ALL OF YOUR TIME HELPING KIDS. WHAT WE DON'T WANT YOU TO DO IS WRITE ARTICLES ABOUT JAZZ ON THE JOB.

HUH!

HOW COULD THAT GUY KNOW ABOUT MY WRITING THAT LETTER? HE WASN'T AT THE SCHOOL. ONE OF MY CO-WORKERS TIPPED HIM OFF.

BUT WHY? IT WAS RAINING YESTERDAY. NO ONE DID ANYTHING BUT SIT AROUND.

THERE WAS NOTHING TO DO. THERE WERE NO KIDS THERE. IS WRITING A LETTER WORSE THAN KIBITZING?

WHY ARE THEY SINGLING ME OUT? I WONDER IF ONE OF THEM DID IT OR ALL OF THEM WENT TO THE SUPERVISOR.

THAT AFTERNOON FINDS ME AT THE PLAYGROUND.

I BETTER NOT TRUST ANY OF THEM. BETTER JUST DO MY JOB AND KEEP AWAY FROM ALL OF 'EM.

WELL, THESE KIDS ARE O.K. THEY'RE QUIET, THEY DON'T FIGHT AND FIND WAYS TO ENTERTAIN THEMSELVES. AT LEAST I LUCKED OUT IN THAT DEPARTMENT.

AS THE WEEKS WENT BY, I FOUND THE PLAYGROUND GIG QUITE PLEASANT.

YOU KIDS DOIN' AWRIGHT? GOT ENOUGH EQUIPMENT FOR THE GAME?

YEAH, WE'RE FINE.

GOOD, GOOD.

SO, LATER ON IN THE SUMMER, I HAD ALMOST FORGOTTEN ABOUT IT, I GOT THIS LETTER FROM MARTIN WILLIAM, EDITOR OF *JAZZ REVIEW*.

HOLY COW! YOU BET I COULD EXPAND IT, AND I DID, RIGHT AWAY.

Dear Mr. Pekar:
    We consider your letter about Fats Navarro potentially the finest article written on Navarro. Would you be able to expand it for publication?

THEN I SENT IT OFF WITH BATED BREATH TO SEE IF IT WOULD BE ACCEPTED.

IT WAS! THEY WERE GOING TO RUN IT IN AN UPCOMING ISSUE! HOW ABOUT THAT! I WAS GOING TO GET PUBLISHED IN A NATIONALLY DISTRIBUTED, VERY WELL RESPECTED JAZZ MAGAZINE. IT WAS THE BEST JAZZ MAGAZINE I EVER WROTE FOR.

AND I WAS ONLY NINETEEN AT THE TIME.

MY PUBLICATION WAS PRETTY WELL RECEIVED. ACTUALLY, A LOT OF GUYS I KNEW WERE TRYING TO GET VARIOUS THINGS INTO PRINT THEN. WHEN I WAS SUCCESSFUL, THEY WERE VERY NICE ABOUT IT, ALTHOUGH I IMAGINE SOME WERE A BIT JEALOUS. THERE WAS A LOT OF COMPETITION IN CLEVELAND'S INTELLECTUAL CIRCLES.

HEY, MAN, I HEARD YOU GOT AN ARTICLE ACCEPTED IN A JAZZ MAGAZINE.

THAT'S GREAT. JUST TERRIFIC.

IT WAS FUNNY, BECAUSE I WASN'T YOUR PHI BETA KAPPA TYPE OR ETHEREAL POET. I WAS A SCHLUB FROM KINSMAN.

SAM and JERRY'S DELI

MY PARENTS WEREN'T VERY IMPRESSED AT ALL. MY FATHER THOUGHT EUROPEAN JEWS WERE SMARTER THAN AMERICAN JEWS. WHATEVER AN AMERICAN DID, IT HAD TO BE TAKEN WITH A GRAIN OF SALT. BESIDES, HE HATED JAZZ.

JAZZ! FEH!

MY MOTHER PROBABLY LOOKED ON THE EVENT MORE OPTIMISTICALLY, BUT SHE, TOO, WASN'T IMPRESSED WITH JAZZ OR PUBLICATION.

THAT'S FINE, BUT REMEMBER, YOU'RE NOT GETTING PAID FOR THIS. IT WON'T SUPPORT YOU.

SO, IN MY ASPIRATIONS, I WENT FROM BEING A FEARED STREET FIGHTER TO AN ADMIRED INTELLECTUAL.

HAVE YOU READ THIS THING BY RIMBAUD WHERE HE...

I WILL SAY THAT I KEPT DOING SOME FIGHTING, THOUGH. ONE OF THE GUYS I BEAT UP WAS FROM A PROMINENT ITALIAN FAMILY, WHO GOT MAD AT ME WHEN I ACCIDENTALLY CUT HIM OFF WITH MY CAR.

HE WOULDN'T ACCEPT MY APOLOGY, SO I HAD TO DUKE IT OUT WITH HIM IN A CHURCH PARKING LOT.

WHEN HE GOT OUT OF HIS CAR, HE TOOK THIS LITTLE BASEBALL BAT WITH HIM AND SWUNG IT AT ME.

I GRABBED IT, TOOK IT AWAY FROM HIM—

—AND HIT HIM OVER THE HEAD WITH IT SEVERAL TIMES—

—BEFORE BREAKING IT.

I FELT GOOD ABOUT BEATING HIM UP, ESPECIALLY WHEN HE CAME OVER TO ME WITH A BAT.

AT THE SAME TIME, IT'S TOO BAD FOR HIM HE DIDN'T REALIZE I WAS A BAD DRIVER AND I REALLY HADN'T DELIBERATELY CUT HIM OFF.

ANYWAY, NOW IT'S SEPTEMBER, 1959. TIME TO GO BACK TO SCHOOL AGAIN. THIS SEMESTER, TOO, I HADN'T CHOSEN ANY COURSES I THOUGHT I'D HAVE A LOT OF TROUBLE WITH. I REALIZED TIME WAS RUNNING OUT THOUGH.

HEY, WHAT'S HAPPENING?

I WENT AROUND FEELING, BY MY STANDARDS, PRETTY UNTROUBLED, HOPING THAT THINGS WOULD KEEP ON BEING O.K. I WENT BY TO TELL MS. WATERMAN I HAD A PIECE ACCEPTED BY THE *JAZZ REVIEW*.

IF YOU HADN'T HELPED WITH THOSE WRITING PROBLEMS I HAD, I DOUBT I'D HAVE EVEN TRIED TO GET SOMETHING PUBLISHED. THANKS A LOT.

BUT WITH ME, DISASTER IS ALWAYS LOOMING. I HAD TAKEN A GEOGRAPHY COURSE, BUT THIS ONE WAS FILLED WITH SHARP, OLDER STUDENTS, NOT THE INDIFFERENT SCHOLARS I WAS USED TO.

NOW, WHAT IS THE GEOGRAPHICAL CONNECTION BETWEEN SPAIN AND NORTH AFRICA?

AND WE WERE ACTUALLY GOING OVER SOME NEW MATERIAL. GEOGRAPHY WASN'T SHAPING UP AS QUITE THE SNAP COURSE I FIGURED IT TO BE.

I THOUGHT I'D COVERED ALL THE STUFF THERE WAS TO KNOW ABOUT GEOGRAPHY IN THE TEN-ZILLION COURSES I TOOK IN HIGH SCHOOL.

BUT WHEN THE FIRST TEST CAME, I HADN'T TAKEN GOOD NOTES IN CLASS, AND I HADN'T STUDIED FOR IT. CONSEQUENTLY, I GOT ONLY A C+. THIS WAS PARTLY DUE TO THE HIGHER GRADE CURVE. MY CLASSMATES MIGHT NOT HAVE HAD PHOTOGRAPHIC MEMORIES, BUT THEY WERE WORKING HARD.

NOW, I KNOW WHAT I'M GOING TO TELL YOU IS GOING TO SEEM INCREDIBLE, BUT BELIEVE ME, IT HAPPENED.

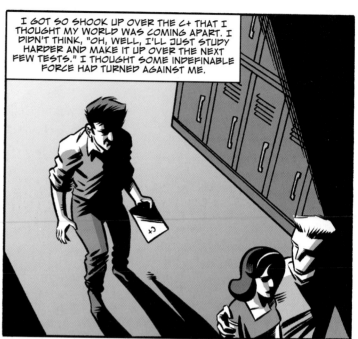

I GOT SO SHOOK UP OVER THE C+ THAT I THOUGHT MY WORLD WAS COMING APART. I DIDN'T THINK, "OH, WELL, I'LL JUST STUDY HARDER AND MAKE IT UP OVER THE NEXT FEW TESTS." I THOUGHT SOME INDEFINABLE FORCE HAD TURNED AGAINST ME.

GEOGRAPHY HAS ALWAYS BEEN THE COURSE I COULD ACE. IF I CAN'T MAKE IT IN GEOGRAPHY, I CAN'T MAKE IT ANYTHING. I'M COMING APART.

IF I DO THIS BAD IN GEOGRAPHY, I'M GOING TO FUCK UP MORE IN THE OTHER CLASSES. I'M GOING TO FLUNK OUT THIS SEMESTER.

I WENT TO A DEAN TO SEE IF I COULD WITHDRAW FROM THE COURSE, BUT I COULDN'T.

NOPE, YOU'VE WAITED TOO LONG.

WELL, THAT'S IT. I'M FINISHED. I'M GONNA QUIT SCHOOL.

OH, COME ON, MR. PEKAR, WHY ARE YOU QUITTING? YOU'RE MAKING A MOUNTAIN OUT OF A MOLEHILL.

BUT THERE WAS NO STOPPING ME. I DID QUIT. I REMEMBER THAT COLD AUTUMN DAY I CAME HOME FROM SCHOOL AND TOLD MY MOTHER I'D QUIT. SOMETHING ELSE SHE DIDN'T UNDERSTAND. I DON'T KNOW IF I DID, EITHER.

OI! WHAT ARE YOU GOING TO DO NOW?

I DUNNO, MA, I JUST CAN'T KEEP QUITTING EVERYTHING.

THEN I GOT REAL MAD AND WENT INTO THE LIVING ROOM AND KICKED THE LEG OFF A CHAIR, JUST BROKE IT IN TWO.

HERSCHEL, WHAT ARE YOU DOING?

NOW, WHILE I'M DOING THIS, MY COUSIN MORT, THE ONE THAT LIVED UPSTAIRS AND WAS ABOUT TWELVE YEARS OLDER THAN ME, THE ONE I LOOKED UPON AS A ROLE MODEL, WAS FESTERING.

MORT WAS MORE OF A STREET PERSON THAN ANYONE ELSE I KNEW IN THE FAMILY. HE WAS ALWAYS HANGING AROUND IN CLUBS AND BARS AT NIGHT; HE DIDN'T SEEM PARTICULARLY INTERESTED IN MARRIAGE. HE'D LOVED THE TRAVEL ASPECT OF BEING IN THE NAVY, LOVED THE NIGHTLIFE IN PLACES LIKE NAPLES AND HAVANA. HE DUG PARTYING, AND HE HAD A REPUTATION AS A TOUGH GUY, TOO.

AFTER HE CAME OUT OF THE NAVY, HE'D GOTTEN JOBS AS A DRAFTSMAN AROUND TOWN, BUT RECENTLY, HE'D BEEN LAID OFF. NOW HE WAS IN KIND OF A QUANDARY. HE LOVED HAVANA AND WAS THINKING ABOUT TAKING OFF AND MOVING TO MIAMI.

I COULDN'T SAY WHAT ELSE WAS IN HIS HEAD, BUT I THOUGHT MAYBE HIS LIFE WAS AT SOME KIND OF CROSSROADS. HE WOULDN'T TALK THAT MUCH TO ME ABOUT IT.

HOW YA DOIN', MORT?

MMMM... I'M OKAY, I GUESS.

A FEW HOURS LATER, MY FATHER CAME HOME FROM WORK. WHEN HE SAW WHAT I'D DONE TO THE CHAIR, HE WAS ENRAGED.

HE BROKE MY CHAIR! HE'S ALWAYS BREAKING MINE STUFF AND NOW HE QUITS SCHOOL AGAIN! GET OUT! GET OUT FROM MINE HOUSE!

I WAS ALARMED. IT WAS FREEZING OUTSIDE AND I HAD NO PLACE TO GO.

I'LL LEAVE, I'LL LEAVE, O.K., BUT DON'T TELL ME I GOT TO GO NOW. I'LL FREEZE TO DEATH.

MY FATHER GRABBED A KITCHEN KNIFE. I DIDN'T KNOW IF HE WAS GONNA COME AFTER ME, OR IF HE WAS JUST TRYING TO DEFEND HIMSELF. HE MIGHT'VE THOUGHT I WAS GOING TO ATTACK.

I GRABBED A CHAIR TO DEFEND MYSELF. THE HOUSE WAS IN AN UPROAR.

MY COUSIN MORT IS UPSTAIRS LISTENING TO ALL OF THIS AND IT'S HAVING GOD ONLY KNOWS WHAT KIND OF EFFECT ON HIM.

HE COMES RUSHING DOWN THE STAIRS.

HE OPENS THE DOOR, SIZES THINGS UP, SEES MY FATHER WITH A KNIFE AND ME WITH A CHAIR.

HE RUSHES INTO THE CROWD AND WINDS UP POKING ME IN THE EYE.

DID HE PUNCH ME IN THE EYE? I DUNNO, I CAN HARDLY FEEL ANYTHING, BUT I THINK HE DID. I GOTTA RETALIATE.

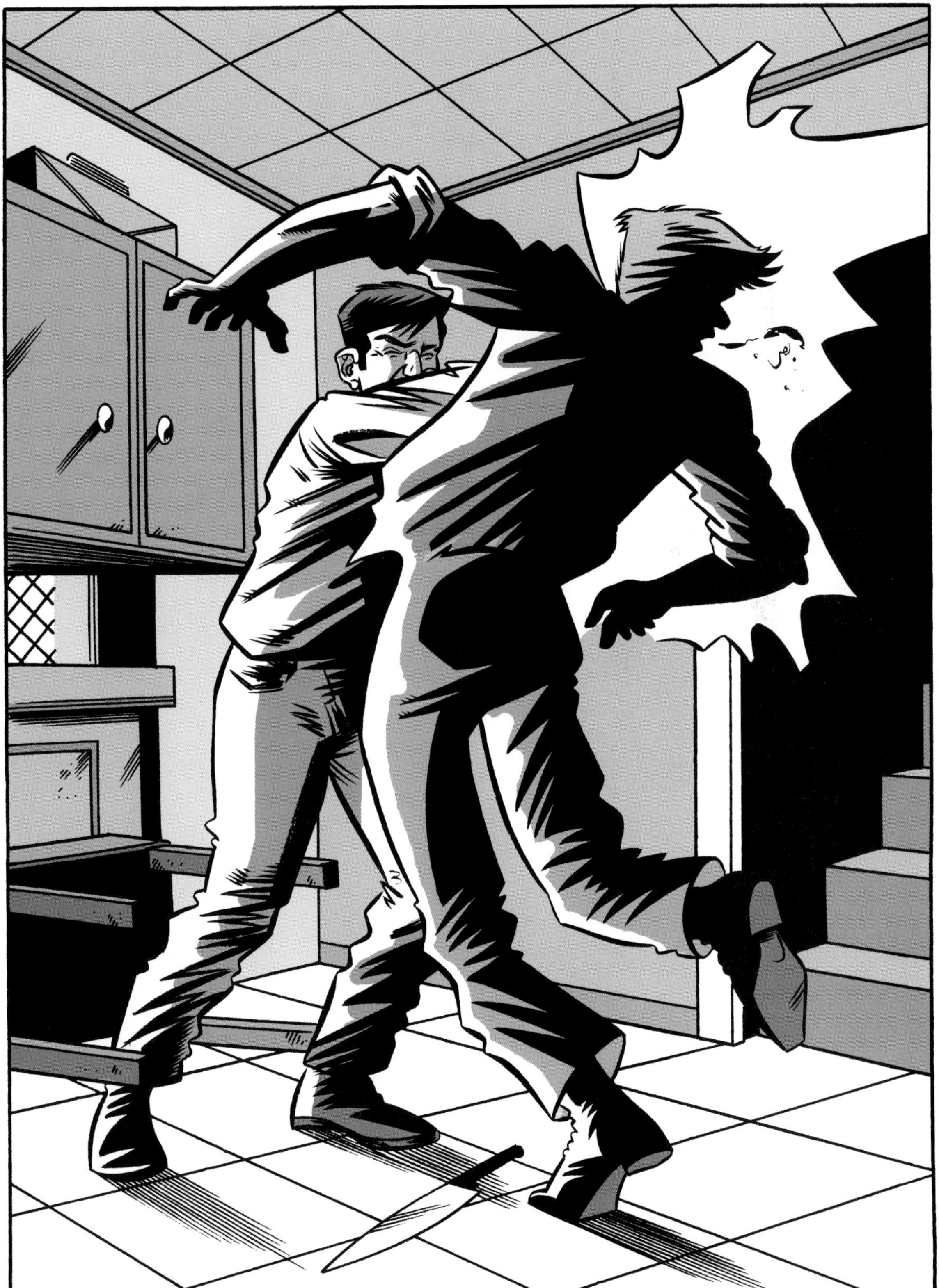

OH, MORTY! I'M SO SORRY...

THAT'S ALL RIGHT. FORGET ABOUT IT.

NOW EVERYBODY'S EXHAUSTED.

LOOK, PA, Y'WANNA GET ME OUTTA THE HOUSE. I THINK I SHOULD GO, TOO. JUST GIVE ME SOME TIME TO FIND A JOB AND I'LL GO.

EVERYBODY DISPERSES AND GOES TO BED.

THE NEXT MORNING...

ALLEN TOLD ME HE COULD GLUE THAT CHAIR LEG TOGETHER.

THAT'S GOOD...LOOK, MA, I'M GOING DOWN TO JEWISH VOCATIONAL TODAY AND SEE IF THEY HAVE ANY KIND OF JOB FOR ME.

IF THEY HAVE SOMETHING, I'M GONNA GET AN APARTMENT AND MOVE OUT. IT'LL BE BEST FOR EVERYBODY.

WELL, WE DO HAVE SOMETHING AT CONCORD RECORD DISTRIBUTORS ON FRANKFORT AVENUE AND WEST SIXTH STREET. IT DOESN'T PAY MUCH-- $50.00 A WEEK.

GUESS THAT'LL BE ENOUGH. I'LL GO APPLY NOW.

I GO DOWN AND GET THE JOB.

WHAT THIS INVOLVES IS SHIPPING CLERK WORK. YOU GET ORDERS FROM OUR CUSTOMERS, PULL THEM, PACK THEM, MAKE AN ENTRY IN THE UPS BOOK, AND SEND THEM.

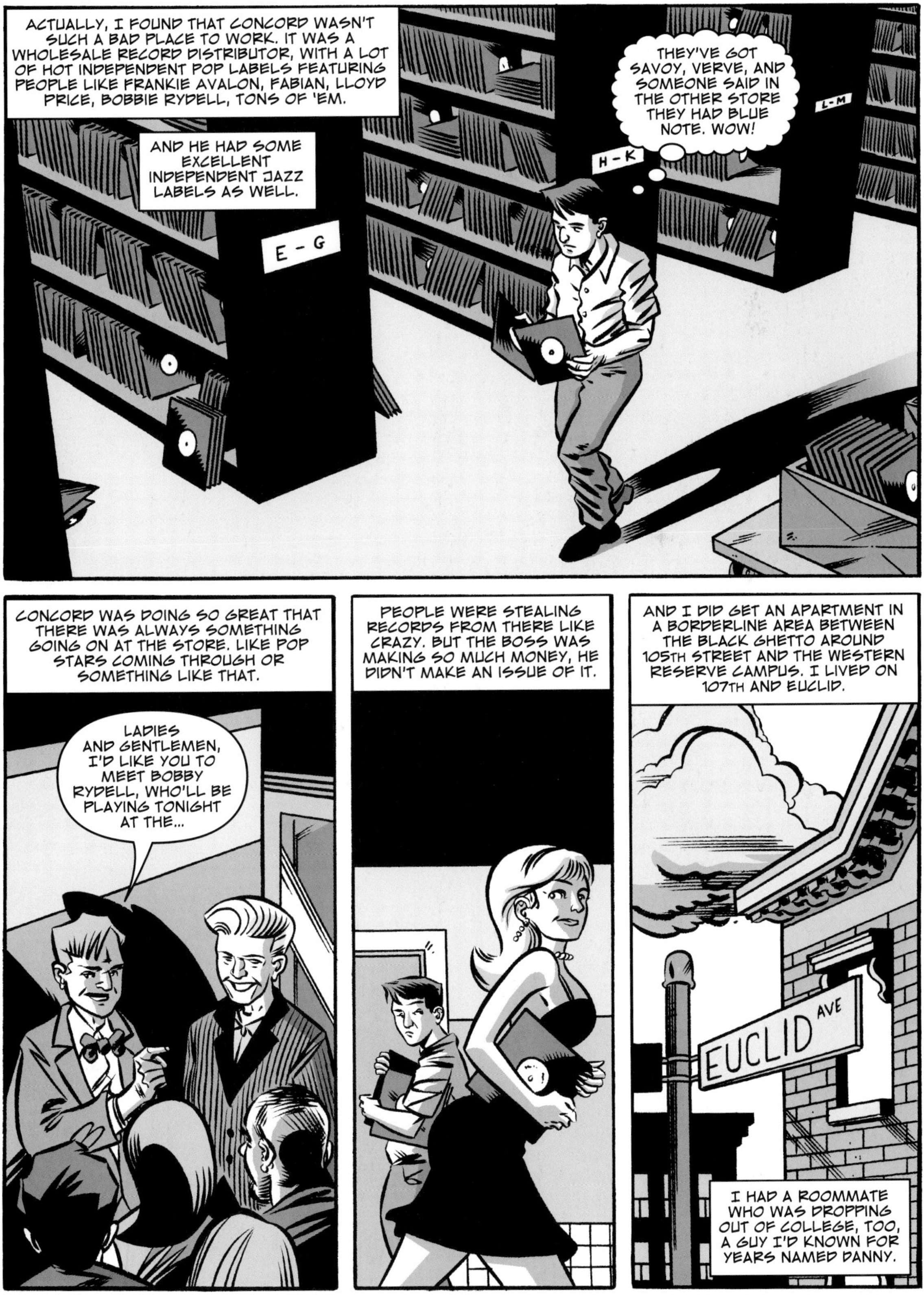
ACTUALLY, I FOUND THAT CONCORD WASN'T SUCH A BAD PLACE TO WORK. IT WAS A WHOLESALE RECORD DISTRIBUTOR, WITH A LOT OF HOT INDEPENDENT POP LABELS FEATURING PEOPLE LIKE FRANKIE AVALON, FABIAN, LLOYD PRICE, BOBBIE RYDELL, TONS OF 'EM.
AND HE HAD SOME EXCELLENT INDEPENDENT JAZZ LABELS AS WELL.
E - G
H - K
L-M
THEY'VE GOT SAVOY, VERVE, AND SOMEONE SAID IN THE OTHER STORE THEY HAD BLUE NOTE. WOW!
CONCORD WAS DOING SO GREAT THAT THERE WAS ALWAYS SOMETHING GOING ON AT THE STORE. LIKE POP STARS COMING THROUGH OR SOMETHING LIKE THAT.
LADIES AND GENTLEMEN, I'D LIKE YOU TO MEET BOBBY RYDELL, WHO'LL BE PLAYING TONIGHT AT THE...
PEOPLE WERE STEALING RECORDS FROM THERE LIKE CRAZY. BUT THE BOSS WAS MAKING SO MUCH MONEY, HE DIDN'T MAKE AN ISSUE OF IT.
AND I DID GET AN APARTMENT IN A BORDERLINE AREA BETWEEN THE BLACK GHETTO AROUND 105TH STREET AND THE WESTERN RESERVE CAMPUS. I LIVED ON 107TH AND EUCLID.
EUCLID AVE
I HAD A ROOMMATE WHO WAS DROPPING OUT OF COLLEGE, TOO, A GUY I'D KNOWN FOR YEARS NAMED DANNY.

DANNY WAS A SMALL, SOFT-SPOKEN GUY WHO WAS REAL INTERESTED IN HIGH FIDELITY EQUIPMENT AND WORKED FOR SOME BROTHERS WHO MANUFACTURED BARGAIN PRICE SPEAKERS AND HAD A COUPLE OF HI-FI EQUIPMENT STORES.

THE APARTMENT WAS REALLY PRETTY NICE FOR OUR PURPOSES. IT WAS A LIVING ROOM, A BEDROOM, A KITCHEN AND A BATHROOM. IT WAS IN THE BASEMENT AND ONLY COST $55.00 A MONTH.

THAT WAS $27.50 APIECE FOR DANNY AND ME. YOU DON'T FIND MANY BETTER DEALS IN LOW-END RENTALS.

AND IT WAS COMFORTABLE, TOO, RIGHT NEXT TO THE FURNACE ROOM. WE MOVED IN DECEMBER AND NEVER FELT A BIT COLD.

IF EITHER DANNY OR I GOT LUCKY AND HAD A GIRL DOWN THERE, THE BEDROOM AND THE LIVING ROOM, WHERE I SLEPT, WERE COMPLETELY SEPARATED BY A WALL.

THE NEIGHBORHOOD, MAN, I COULD SAY ALL KINDS OF THINGS ABOUT THE TWO NEIGHBORHOODS WE LIVED BETWEEN.

TO THE EAST WAS THE 105TH AND EUCLID AREA. ITS STORES WERE FAR MORE SEEDY THAN THEY HAD BEEN 15 YEARS AGO AND IT WAS BEING ENVELOPED IN THE BLACK GHETTO AREAS THAT SURROUNDED IT.

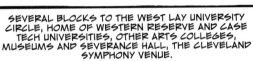

THERE WERE ALSO SOME GOOD CHEAP RESTAURANTS IN THE AREA, FIVE MOVIE THEATRES AND SEVERAL JAZZ CLUBS, SO IT WAS STILL A PRETTY EXCITING PLACE, ALTHOUGH IT HAS SINCE BEEN WIPED AWAY BY URBAN RENEWAL.

SEVERAL BLOCKS TO THE WEST LAY UNIVERSITY CIRCLE, HOME OF WESTERN RESERVE AND CASE TECH UNIVERSITIES, OTHER ARTS COLLEGES, MUSEUMS AND SEVERANCE HALL, THE CLEVELAND SYMPHONY VENUE.

SO, I WAS LIVING IN AN AREA WHERE THERE WERE A VARIETY OF INTERESTING CULTURAL ACTIVITIES GOING ON. CRIME WAS COMMON IN BOTH SECTIONS, HOWEVER.

DANNY AND I USED TO SPEND A LOT OF TIME IN THE NEIGHBORHOODS, TAKING IN CONCERTS, MOVIES, PLAYS AND ART EXHIBITS. CULTURALLY, IT WAS PROBABLY THE RICHEST SECTION OF CLEVELAND, ALTHOUGH, AS I SAID, CRIME-RIDDEN.

AS FOR MY RECORD DISTRIBUTOR'S GIG, IT WAS O.K. FOR A WHILE. I MADE SURE TO KEEP MY NOSE TO THE GRINDSTONE AT FIRST--IT WAS A GIG I NEEDED TO HOLD ONTO.

INITIALLY, THE OWNER WAS IMPRESSED WITH MY ASSIDUOUSNESS, AND AFTER A COUPLE OF WEEKS HE CALLED A MEETING IN WHICH HE AWARDED ME A RAISE OF $2.50 PER WEEK--AS IF THIS WAS ENOUGH TO SPUR EVERYONE IN THE PLACE TO KNOCK THEMSELVES OUT FOR HIM.

NOW I REALIZE PAY FOR SHIPPING CLERKS IS LOW, BUT I'M WILLING TO GIVE RAISES FOR HARD WORK.

ACTUALLY, MANY OF HIS OTHER EMPLOYEES WERE ROBBING HIM BLIND, PULLING CARS UP TO THE LOADING DOCK, FILLING THEM WITH HUNDREDS OF DOLLARS' WORTH OF RECORDS AND SELLING THEM ON THE STREET. THEY DIDN'T NEED HIS $2.50.

FOR A WHILE, IT WAS A VERY PLEASANT WAY TO LIVE FOR ME. THE WORK WAS EASY, THE APARTMENT COMFORTABLE, THE NEIGHBORHOOD FULL OF ACTIVITY.

I ALSO DID A LOT OF WRITING FOR THE *JAZZ REVIEW*, WHICH WAS VERY SUPPORTIVE OF MY WORK, ESPECIALLY WHEN I DEALT WITH MUSICIANS WHO HAD BEEN IGNORED AND DESERVED GREATER RECOGNITION.

GRADUALLY, I GOT TO SCREWING AROUND LIKE THE OTHER GUYS, THOUGH. WE HAD A LOT OF FUN ON THE JOB AT THE OWNER'S EXPENSE. HE TOOK A LOT OF CRAP FROM ME BECAUSE HE, TOO, WAS JEWISH.

C'MON, HARVEY. YOU GOT OFF TO A GOOD START, BUT NOW YOU'RE SLIPPING.

I USED TO INSULT HIM FREQUENTLY IN FRONT OF HIS CO-WORKERS AND EVEN BIG SHOTS WHO CAME INTO THE OFFICE FOR RECORDS.

DO YOU EXPECT US TO BELIEVE THAT BULLSHIT?

ONCE, THE HEAD OF CLEVELAND'S CITY COUNCIL CAME IN TO PICK UP, HE BEING HUNGARIAN, A BUNCH OF RECORDS BY A HUNGARIAN VIOLINIST.

IN THE MEANTIME, I WAS SCREWING AROUND IN THE BACK OF THE STORE WITH A BOOMERANG LEFT OVER FROM THE PROMOTION OF AN AUSTRALIAN POP MUSIC SINGER.

I THREW THE BOOMERANG THE LENGTH OF THE ROOM. IT BENT INTO A WINDOW AND HIT THE HUNGARIAN POLITICIAN, WHO WAS SMOKING A BIG CIGAR AND WEARING A TEN-GALLON HAT, RIGHT IN THE STOMACH AS HE WAS LAYING DOWN A WAD OF BILLS FOR THE RECORDS.

FORTUNATELY, HE WAS WEARING A HEAVY COAT AND WASN'T HURT BY THE BOOMERANG WHEN IT HIT HIM. HE WAS MORE SURPRISED THAN ANYTHING ELSE, AND DIDN'T COMPLAIN WHEN THE INCIDENT HAPPENED. BUT I SHOULD'VE REALIZED THAT I WAS LUCKY TO GET AWAY WITH WHAT I DID.

MEANWHILE, I, OF ALL PEOPLE, FOUND A GIRLFRIEND. THIS FRIEND OF DANNY'S AND HIS DATE STOPPED OVER TO OUR APARTMENT ONE EVENING BEFORE THEY WENT OUT TO A SHOW.

THEY WERE ABOUT TO LEAVE, WHEN THE GIRL, ELLEN, CAME OVER TO THE BED I WAS LYING ON AND STARTED KISSING AND CARESSING ME. NEEDLESS TO SAY, I WAS PLEASANTLY SURPRISED.

WHEN IT CAME TIME FOR HER TO LEAVE WITH HER DATE, SHE DIDN'T, PREFERRING TO SPEND THE NIGHT WITH ME.

GO TO THE MOVIE. I'M STAYING WITH HARVEY.

I'M NOT SURE WHY SHE WAS ATTRACTED TO ME, BUT WE STARTED HANGING AROUND TOGETHER AND HAVING A GOOD TIME, UNTIL HER WINTER VACATION WAS OVER AND SHE HAD TO GO BACK TO OHIO STATE, WHERE SHE WAS A SENIOR.

SHE'D COME BACK SOME WEEKENDS, THOUGH, AND WE'D HAVE A GREAT TIME. ONCE, SHE MADE THE FOLLOWING SUGGESTION:

WE OUGHT TO GET MARRIED, YOU KNOW.

WELL, I DIDN'T TAKE HER REMARKS TOO SERIOUSLY AT THE TIME, BUT I DID LATER.

SHE WAS A VERY BRIGHT WOMAN AND TREATED ME, FOR A WHILE, WITH A LOT OF RESPECT.

I REALLY LIKE THAT NEW ARTICLE YOU WROTE.

SO, EVERYTHING LOOKED PRETTY GOOD FOR ME FOR THE TIME BEING, BUT THEN, AS USUAL, I HAD TO GO AND SCREW IT UP.

I HAD BEEN VERY ABUSIVE TO THE OWNER OF CONCORD AND EVEN TO SOME OF HIS CUSTOMERS OF LATE, AND I KNEW THAT I WAS PUSHING MY LUCK, SO I DECIDED TO SHUT UP.

THERE HE IS, BRAGGING AGAIN. WELL, I BETTER NOT SAY ANYTHING ABOUT IT. I'VE BEEN TOO INSULTING AS IT IS.

BUT ONE DAY WE WERE KIDDING AROUND AND I MADE WHAT WAS MEANT AS A JOKING REFERENCE TO SOME SEXUAL MATTERS.

THAT MUST HAVE REALLY GOTTEN TO HIM, BECAUSE, THE NEXT DAY, I WAS TOLD I WAS CANNED. WOULD I NEVER LEARN?

I KNOW I HAD IT COMING. I WENT OUT AND BEGAN TO LOOK FOR MORE WORK RIGHT AWAY.

HELP WANTED

IT WAS EARLY SPRING, A GOOD TIME FOR LOOKING FOR SEASONAL WORK IN THE LOCAL BREWERIES.

I WENT DOWN TO THE LOCAL UNION AND MADE OUT AN APPLICATION. IN THE PAST, I HADN'T GOTTEN THESE BREWERY WORKER JOBS BECAUSE WHEN THEY ASKED ME...

WHO SENT YA DOWN?

I WOULDN'T HAVE AN ANSWER. NO CONNECTIONS, NO JOB.

NOBODY, I JUST THOUGHT YOU WERE HIRING.

THIS TIME, WHEN HE ASKED ME THE QUESTION, I GAVE THE UNION BOSS AN ANSWER. I NAMED AN ITALIAN GUY WHO WAS A FRIEND OF DANNY'S AND A DISTANT RELATIVE OF THE UNION GUY.

JOE AMATO, HUH? WHERE YOU KNOW HIM FROM?

JOE AMATO.

OH, FROM AROUND 154TH AND KINSMAN. SOMETIMES I SEE 'IM AT SAM AND JERRY'S.

WELL, O.K., WE GOT AN OPENING AT CARLING'S BREWERY, BUT WHEN YOU GO OVER THERE, I WANT YOU TO WORK HARD. THE BOYS FROM KINSMAN THINK THEY CAN GET BY WITHOUT WORKING.

OH, NA, NA! I'LL WORK HARD. I DON'T GOOF AROUND.

AND I DID WORK PRETTY HARD. AT LEAST, I DIDN'T MESS AROUND LIKE I HAD ON OTHER GIGS.

BUT REALLY, THERE WASN'T MUCH TO WORK HARD AT ON THE JOB. I HAD TO BE ON A PRODUCTION LINE MOST OF THE TIME WATCHING THE BEER BOTTLES GO PAST A LIGHT AND LOOKING FOR ONES THAT WERE UNCAPPED OR HAD FOREIGN MATERIAL IN THE BEER, LIKE CIGARETTES OR PIECES OF PAPER.

THE JOB WAS BORING, BUT I'D GOTTEN PAST THE POINT WHERE I EXPECTED ANYTHING ELSE.

I WONDER IF I'LL EVER FIND A JOB I ENJOY. PROBABLY NOT.

ANOTHER THING WAS THAT THEY PUT ME ON SECOND SHIFT, FROM 4:00 PM TO MIDNIGHT. I DIDN'T LIKE GOING TO WORK SO LATE--IT BROKE UP THE DAY. BUT THE MONEY WAS GOOD BY MY STANDARDS--$2.50 AN HOUR.

GOING HOME FROM WORK AT MIDNIGHT. THAT DON'T SEEM NATURAL.

BUS STOP

IT WAS AN ITALIAN-RUN UNION, BUT THERE WERE A LOT OF JEWISH WORKERS AT THE PLANT IN 1959, SINCE JEWS AND ITALIANS LIVED NEAR EACH OTHER IN THOSE DAYS.

HEY, HYMIE.

HEY, SCHLOMIE.

BUT IN THE LATE 1950'S, THERE WERE STILL A FEW WORKING CLASS JEWS AROUND--GUYS WHO WERE IMMIGRANTS OR NOT REAL BRIGHT, OR UNLUCKY.

AFTER I GET OFF WORK, I'M GOING DOWN 105TH AND GET SMASHED.

I HATE TO HEAR YOU SAY THAT, MORRIS. A SHICKER* IS SUPPOSED TO BE A GOY, REMEMBER?

*SHICKER: DRUNK

OLD YIDDISH SONG: OY OY OY! A SHICKER IS A GOY!

WHEN ELLEN CAME UP FROM OHIO STATE, WE'D HAVE A GOOD TIME. NOW THAT I WAS MAKING $100 A WEEK, MONEY WAS NO PROBLEM.

WE'D GO TO THE ART MUSEUM OR MOVIES. AND WE ALWAYS ATE GOOD, ESPECIALLY AT THESE TWO DELICATESSENS ON 105TH AND EUCLID.

CORNED BEEF AND FRENCH FRIES. IT DOESN'T GET ANY BETTER THAN THAT.

THE THING WAS, I KNEW I WAS ON BORROWED TIME. THE BREWERY USED TO DO A LOT OF HIRING AND FIRING DURING EVEN THE BUSY SEASON. THE MORE PEOPLE THEY LET GO, THE MORE THEY HAD TO REPLACE 'EM, AND NEW EMPLOYEES HADDA PAY AN INITIATION FEE OF $100 TO THE UNION, SO FIRST HIRED MIGHT BE FIRST LAID OFF.

HOPE THEY KEEP ME TILL THE END OF THE SUMMER.

WELL, I WAS WAITING FOR THAT, AND, AFTER SEVERAL MONTHS, IT HAPPENED. I WAS LAID OFF. I HAD A REACTION THEN I HAD NEVER HAD BEFORE. I GOT TO FEELING REAL DEPENDENT.

OH, NO, I'VE BEEN LAID OFF!

I TOOK A BUS DOWN TO COLUMBUS, WHERE ELLEN WAS JUST FINISHING UP HER SEMESTER, AND I ASKED HER TO MARRY ME. SHE WAS SURPRISED, BUT NOT OVERJOYED. SHE ACCEPTED, BUT KIND OF RELUCTANTLY. I WAS LOOKING FOR HER TO BE REAL HAPPY ABOUT IT, BUT, EVIDENTLY, SHE DIDN'T VALUE ME, OR HER OWN LIFE, AS MUCH AS I THOUGHT.

YOU'LL DO IT? GREAT!

YEAH, I WILL.

I HAD SOME DOUGH SAVED UP AND I GOT UNEMPLOYMENT, SO WE WERE ABLE TO MAKE IT ON THAT. WE MOVED INTO A ROW HOUSE ACROSS FROM WHERE I WAS LIVING. THE RENT WAS ONLY $79.00 PER MONTH.

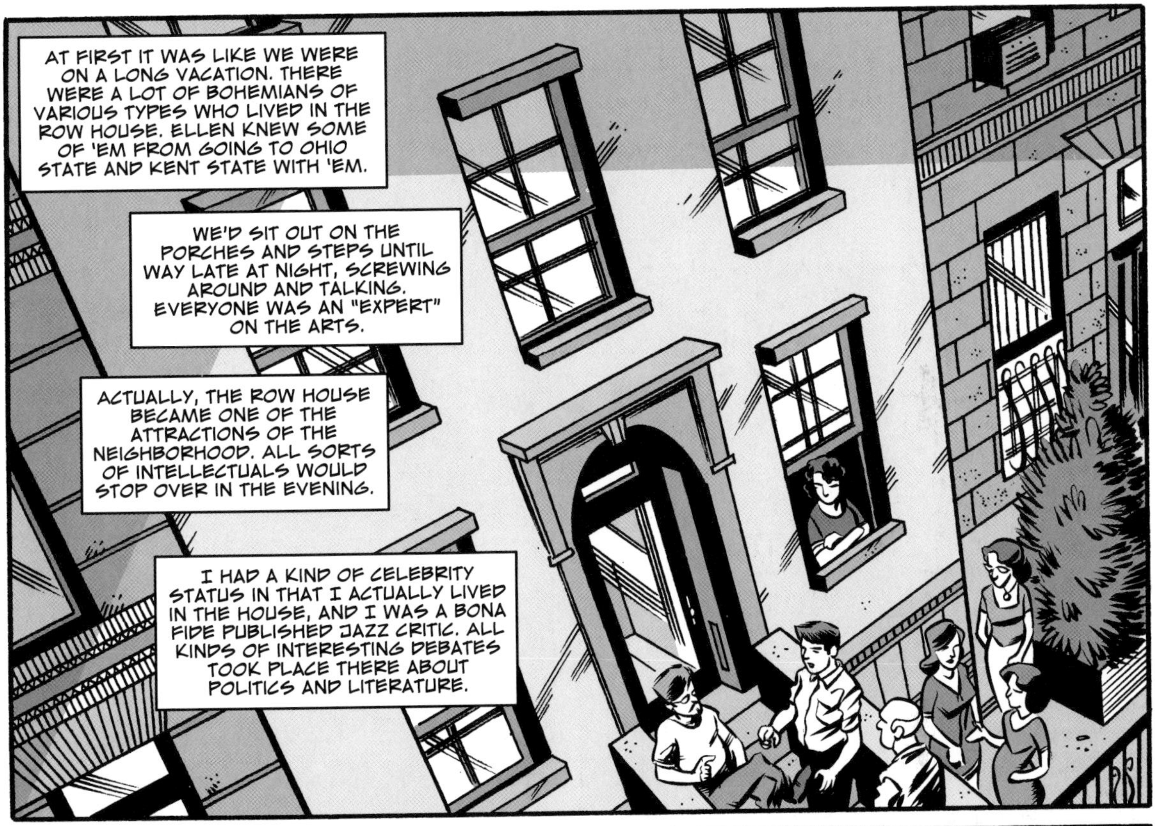
AT FIRST IT WAS LIKE WE WERE ON A LONG VACATION. THERE WERE A LOT OF BOHEMIANS OF VARIOUS TYPES WHO LIVED IN THE ROW HOUSE. ELLEN KNEW SOME OF 'EM FROM GOING TO OHIO STATE AND KENT STATE WITH 'EM.
WE'D SIT OUT ON THE PORCHES AND STEPS UNTIL WAY LATE AT NIGHT, SCREWING AROUND AND TALKING. EVERYONE WAS AN "EXPERT" ON THE ARTS.
ACTUALLY, THE ROW HOUSE BECAME ONE OF THE ATTRACTIONS OF THE NEIGHBORHOOD. ALL SORTS OF INTELLECTUALS WOULD STOP OVER IN THE EVENING.
I HAD A KIND OF CELEBRITY STATUS IN THAT I ACTUALLY LIVED IN THE HOUSE, AND I WAS A BONA FIDE PUBLISHED JAZZ CRITIC. ALL KINDS OF INTERESTING DEBATES TOOK PLACE THERE ABOUT POLITICS AND LITERATURE.

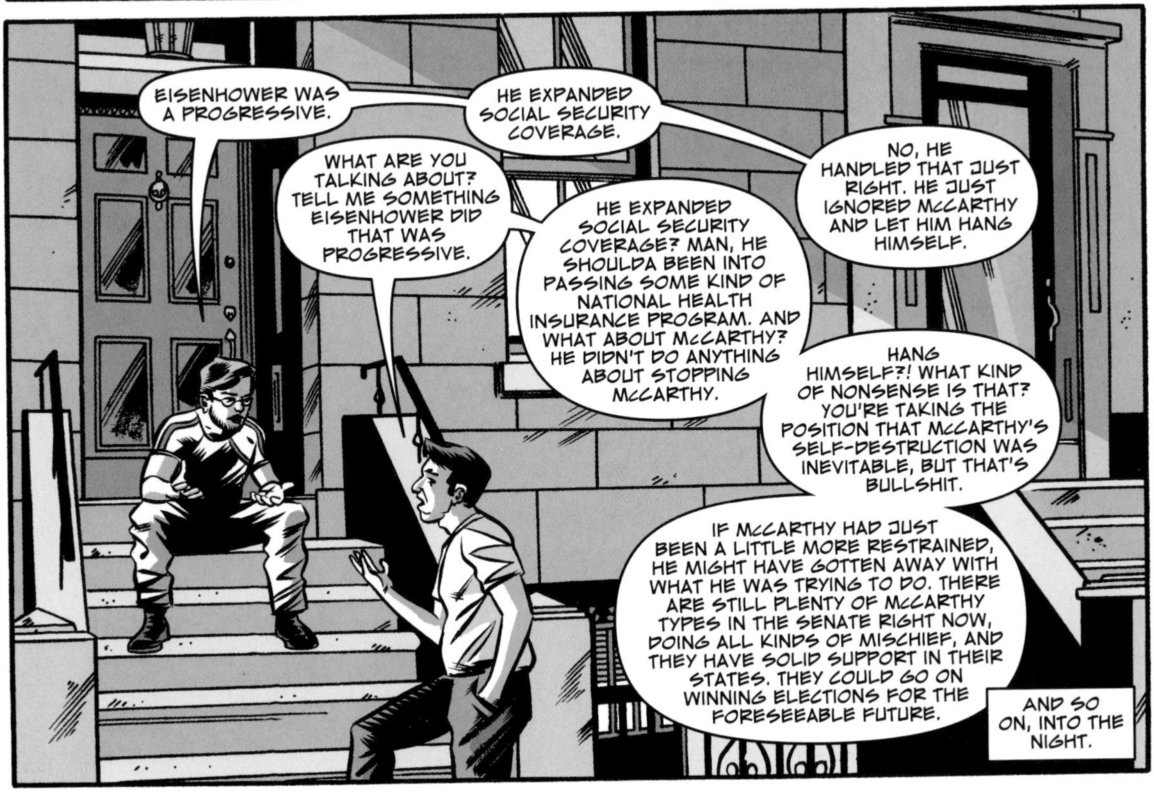
EISENHOWER WAS A PROGRESSIVE.
HE EXPANDED SOCIAL SECURITY COVERAGE.
WHAT ARE YOU TALKING ABOUT? TELL ME SOMETHING EISENHOWER DID THAT WAS PROGRESSIVE.
HE EXPANDED SOCIAL SECURITY COVERAGE? MAN, HE SHOULDA BEEN INTO PASSING SOME KIND OF NATIONAL HEALTH INSURANCE PROGRAM. AND WHAT ABOUT McCARTHY? HE DIDN'T DO ANYTHING ABOUT STOPPING McCARTHY.
NO, HE HANDLED THAT JUST RIGHT. HE JUST IGNORED McCARTHY AND LET HIM HANG HIMSELF.
HANG HIMSELF?! WHAT KIND OF NONSENSE IS THAT? YOU'RE TAKING THE POSITION THAT McCARTHY'S SELF-DESTRUCTION WAS INEVITABLE, BUT THAT'S BULLSHIT.
IF McCARTHY HAD JUST BEEN A LITTLE MORE RESTRAINED, HE MIGHT HAVE GOTTEN AWAY WITH WHAT HE WAS TRYING TO DO. THERE ARE STILL PLENTY OF McCARTHY TYPES IN THE SENATE RIGHT NOW, DOING ALL KINDS OF MISCHIEF, AND THEY HAVE SOLID SUPPORT IN THEIR STATES. THEY COULD GO ON WINNING ELECTIONS FOR THE FORESEEABLE FUTURE.
AND SO ON, INTO THE NIGHT.

THERE WAS ALWAYS SOME KIND OF DECENT JAZZ TO LISTEN TO IN THE NEIGHBORHOOD, TOO, PARTICULARLY AT THE CLUB 100, WHERE ROLAND KIRK PLAYED, AND ALSO A FINE LOCAL TENOR PLAYER, JOE ALEXANDER.

I GOT A GIG AS AN ALL-AROUND FLUNKY CLERK FOR THE WESTERN RESERVE UNIVERSITY DOCUMENTATION CENTER. THEY WERE DOING EXPERIMENTATION WITH COMPUTERS, THE PROGRAM WAS IN TRANSITION, BUT I KEPT THE GIG FOR TWO YEARS--THAT'S LONGER THAN I EXPECTED. THEY USED THESE HUGE COMPUTERS WITH PUNCH CARDS AND MAGNETIC TAPE.

ACTUALLY, WHEN THEY STARTED LAYING OFF CLERKS, THEY TRIED TO ELEVATE ME TO COMPUTER OPERATOR SO I COULD STAY THERE, BUT YOU KNOW ABOUT ME AND MACHINES; I MADE A MESS OF IT.

I MADE A LOT OF INTERESTING ACQUAINTANCES IN THOSE DAYS. A LOT OF FOREIGN-BORN PEOPLE WERE WORKING ON THE PROJECT, SO I GOT TO SEE THE WORLD THROUGH THEIR EYES.

ONE OF THE GUYS WHO WORKED THERE WAS AMISH. HE HAD BROKEN AWAY FROM HIS COMMUNITY, THOUGH, AND WAS MAJORING IN ENGLISH AT COLLEGE. I THINK HE EVENTUALLY GOT HIS PH.D. FINE GUY, AND A REAL HARD WORKER.

THAT LIFE WAS JUST TOO HARD FOR ME, HARVEY.

I ALSO HAD A JOB WORKING AS A SALESMAN IN ONE OF THE HI-FI STORES WHERE DANNY WAS NOW PRETTY HIGH UP IN THE CHAIN OF COMMAND.

WE THINK THESE SPEAKERS ARE TOPS AS FAR AS A DOLLAR VALUE IN THE SPEAKER LINE IS CONCERNED.

THAT WAS A LAUGH. I DIDN'T KNOW SHIT ABOUT HI-FI OR ELECTRONICS. BUT I WAS DESPERATE FOR MONEY AND DID A REAL GOOD JOB, UNTIL THE HI-FI MAGAZINES STARTED TAKING THEIR SPEAKERS APART AND WROTE THAT THEY WERE NOT THE SCIENTIFIC BREAKTHROUGHS THEY WERE CLAIMED TO BE IN ADVERTISEMENTS.

THE JOBS I HAD KEPT ME GOING, ALTHOUGH THEY DIDN'T LEAD TO ANYTHING. BUT I DID MAKE SOME PROGRESS IN THE EARLY 1960'S IN TERMS OF WRITING AND MEETING PEOPLE.

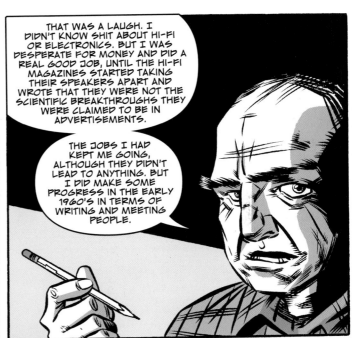

THE *JAZZ REVIEW*, AS FINE A JAZZ MAGAZINE AS WAS EVER PUBLISHED, FOLDED IN 1961. IT JUST WENT OVER THE HEADS OF ORDINARY FANS.

BUT IT HAD SUCH A GOOD REPUTATION AMONG EDITORS AND KNOWLEDGEABLE FANS THAT I DIDN'T HAVE ANY TROUBLE PICKING UP WORK AT THE ENGLISH MAGAZINES, *THE JAZZ JOURNAL* AND *JAZZ MONTHLY*.

AND THEN IRA GITLER CAME THROUGH FOR ME AGAIN. HE RECOMMENDED ME FOR THE REVIEWING STAFF OF *DOWNBEAT* AND I GOT THE GIG. IT PAID FOUR DOLLARS A REVIEW, THE FIRST TIME I'D EVER BEEN PAID FOR WRITING ABOUT JAZZ.

NOT TOO MANY PEOPLE HAD HEARD OF *JAZZ REVIEW*, BUT *DOWNBEAT* WAS THE BIGGEST OF ALL JAZZ MAGAZINES, SO I GUESS I GOT A LITTLE MORE PRESTIGE.

CONGRATULATIONS. EVEN I'VE HEARD OF *DOWNBEAT*.

IN 1962, I MET A NINETEEN-YEAR-OLD COLLECTOR WHO'D JUST MOVED INTO TOWN FROM PHILADELPHIA, BY THE NAME OF ROBERT CRUMB. HE WAS A CARTOONIST TOO, AND HIS BUDDY URGED ME TO LOOK AT HIS STUFF.

YOU SHOULD CHECK HIS WORK OUT, HARVEY. IT'S GREAT.

I DID AND IT WAS.

MAN, THIS BIG YUM YUM BOOK IS GREAT. IT'S A REAL COMIC BOOK NOVEL. I CAN SEE WHERE THE SATIRE IN IT HAS BEEN INFLUENCED BY MAD, BUT IT GOES FURTHER THAN MAD.

R. CRUMB'S THE YUM YUM BOOK

WHERE DO YOU WANT TO PUBLISH THIS THING ANYWAY?

OH, I DUNNO. IT'S JUST AN EXPERIMENT.

IT'S AN EXPERIMENT, BUT I CAN TELL YOU RIGHT NOW IT'S AN EXPERIMENT THAT WORKS. YOU SHOULD DO SOMETHING WITH THIS.

CRUMB GOT HIMSELF A JOB AS A COLOR SEPARATOR AT THE AMERICAN GREETING CARD CO. IN CLEVELAND.

BUT IT WASN'T TOO LONG BEFORE HE'D WORKED HIS WAY UP TO ONE OF THEIR MAJOR CARD ILLUSTRATORS.

HE GOT SO GOOD THAT HE DIDN'T EVEN HAVE TO SHOW UP AT THE JOB TO DO HIS WORK. HE COULD FLY ALL OVER THE GLOBE AND SEND IN HIS CARD ILLUSTRATIONS BY MAIL AND THAT'D BE GOOD ENOUGH TO SATISFY THE PEOPLE AT AMERICAN GREETINGS.

AS A MATTER OF FACT, HE DID TAKE A TRIP TO BULGARIA IN 1965 OR SO AND DID A CARTOON STORY ON BULGARIA FOR *HELP*, THIS MAGAZINE THAT WAS EDITED BY HARVEY KURTZMAN, THE EDITOR OF MAD.

WOW, THERE'S SOME CRUMB STUFF IN HERE.

THEN, IN THE WINTER OF 1966-1967, HE WENT OUT TO SAN FRANCISCO, AND BECAME PART OF THE HIPPIE SCENE THERE.

IN FACT, HE SOON BECAME ONE OF THE LEADING FIGURES IN THE UNDERGROUND CARTOON MOVEMENT, WHICH HAD ARISEN WITH THE HIPPIE CULTURE.

MAN, CRUMB'S PICTURE IS IN THIS MAGAZINE.

SO I WAS FOLLOWING ALL THIS--SEE. I WAS FOLLOWING THE WORK OF CRUMB AND THE OTHER EARLY UNDERGROUND CARTOONISTS, FROM CLEVELAND, WHERE, IN 1965, I FINALLY GOT A JOB BACK WITH THE FEDERAL GOVERNMENT, WHICH I STAYED WITH UNTIL I RETIRED.

I LEARNED MY LESSON. I'M NEVER LEAVING THE FEDERAL GOVERNMENT.

I LIKED UNDERGROUND COMICS IMMENSELY; STILL IT OCCURRED TO ME THAT EVEN MORE COULD BE DONE WITH THEM.

LIKE, UNDERGROUND COMICS WERE OFTEN WRITTEN ABOUT THE BOHEMIAN LIFE STYLE.

HEY, MAN, GOT ANY MORE A' THAT WEED?

BUT IT DIDN'T HAVE TO BE THAT WAY ALL THE TIME. UNDERGROUND COMICS HAD ALREADY PROVED THAT COMICS COULD APPEAL TO ADULTS. THEY WERE AS GOOD AN ART FORM AS ANY THAT EXISTED. COMICS ARE WORDS AND PICTURES--YOU CAN DO ANYTHING WITH WORDS AND PICTURES.

BOY, I WONDER WHY NO ONE'S TRIED ANYTHING MORE AMBITIOUS WITH COMICS BEFORE. THEY'RE SUCH A GREAT MEDIUM.

THE FABULOUS FURRY

SO I THOUGHT, WHY COULDN'T I WRITE ABOUT EVERYDAY QUOTIDIAN SUBJECTS IN COMICS? WHY COULDN'T COMICS BE ABOUT THE LIVES OF WORKING STIFFS? WE'RE AS INTERESTING AND FUNNY AS ANYONE ELSE.

I GET AS SHOOK UP OVER MONEY AS RICH PEOPLE, ONLY IT'S LESS MONEY.

AS TIME WENT ON, I DEVELOPED MY THEORIES ABOUT COMICS MORE AND MORE. I DECIDED THAT COMIC STORIES COULD BE AS LONG AND COMPLEX AS PROSE STORIES.

MAN, TO ACCOMMODATE A STORY LIKE THAT WOULD TAKE THIRTY-FIVE PAGES. BUT, WHY NOT? GIVE IT AS MANY PAGES AS IT NEEDS.

THERE WAS NOTHING INTRINSICALLY LIMITED ABOUT COMICS, ONLY THE WAY THEY WERE BEING USED.

LOOK AT THIS. NOTHING BUT SUPER HERO CRAP.

GREEN LANTERN

WONDER WOMAN

HULK

DETECTIVE COMICS

ACTION COMICS

SHAZAM!

AND, AS YOU PROBABLY KNOW, I FINALLY GOT AROUND TO WRITING COMIC SCRIPTS IN STORYBOARD FORM, AND ROBERT CRUMB AND OTHER FINE ARTISTS ILLUSTRATED THEM FOR ME.

HEY, HARVEY, I REALLY LIKE THIS.

THANKS, MAN. YEAH, I WAS HAPPY WITH IT, TOO.

AMERICAN SPLENDOR

MY AMERICAN SPLENDOR COMICS HAVE BEEN AROUND SINCE 1976 NOW, AND I'LL KEEP ON DOING THEM FOR AS LONG AS I CAN. A MOVIE WAS BASED ON AMERICAN SPLENDOR. RELEASED IN 2003, IT WON SOME PRIZES, LIKE THE SUNDANCE AND CANNES AWARDS.

IT'S BEEN A LONG, WEIRD TRIP FROM MY DAYS AS A SCHOOL KID FIGHTING ALL OVER THE PLACE TO DOING JAZZ CRITICISM AND FINALLY COMICS, AND SEEING MY PICTURE IN THE NEW YORK TIMES AND USA TODAY.

I CAN'T BELIEVE THIS IS HAPPENING.

PEKAR'S AMERICAN SPLENDOR ONE OF TOP FILMS OF THE YEAR

AND THE WINNER IS... AMERICAN SPLENDOR!

SUNDANCE

MY PRIORITIES HAVE SHIFTED A LOT OVER THE YEARS, FROM WANTING TO BE KNOWN AS A TOUGH GUY TO BEING PRAISED AS A WRITER.

THE "GENIUS" AT WORK.

BUT THEN THERE'S THINGS THAT HAVEN'T CHANGED, MAINLY HAVING TO DO WITH MY INSECURITY.

I STILL NEED RECOGNITION FROM OTHERS REGARDING MY ACCOMPLISHMENTS. I CAN'T BE SATISFIED WITH ONLY ME HAVING A GOOD OPINION OF MYSELF.

BOY, I'D A' THOUGHT SOMEONE WOULD'VE WRITTEN ME A LETTER ABOUT MY NEW BOOK BY NOW.

BEYOND THAT, I'M ALWAYS INSECURE ABOUT MONEY. I'M RETIRED NOW, AND GET A SMALL PENSION FROM THE FEDERAL GOVERNMENT. I NEED, ON TOP OF THAT, MONEY FROM FREE-LANCE WRITING GIGS, COMICS AND PROSE, TO HAVE A DECENT INCOME.

I'D BETTER CALL THE FREE TIMES AN' ASK WHETHER THEY WANT ME TO WRITE SOME JAZZ REVIEWS FOR 'EM.

MY COMIC SALES HAVE ALWAYS BEEN SMALL, EXCEPT WHEN THE MOVIE CAME OUT AND A COMPANION AMERICAN SPLENDOR BOOK WAS PUBLISHED AND DID VERY WELL. MONEY FROM THE MOVIE IS EARMARKED FOR MY KID'S EDUCATION, THOUGH. I JUST HOPE WE CAN ALL GET THROUGH.

NOW, AS A RESULT OF THOSE GOOD RECENT BOOK SALES, I HAVE BEEN ABLE TO GET COMIC BOOK WRITING GIGS FROM A COUPLE OF COMPANIES FOR ABOUT FIVE BOOKS.

WOW, I SURE HOPE THIS KEEPS UP.

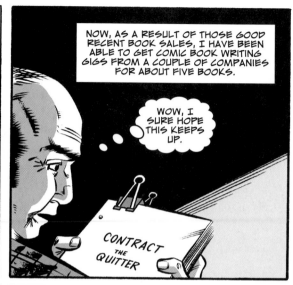

CONTRACT THE QUITTER

BUT I'M SCARED ABOUT HOW THOSE BOOKS WILL BE RECEIVED BY THE PUBLIC. WILL THEY GO UNNOTICED BY THE PUBLIC AS MY PRE-MOVIE BOOKS WERE, OR DO I HAVE A LARGER CORE AUDIENCE?

I'M AFRAID TO LOOK AT THE REVIEWS.

IN OTHER WORDS, CAN I MAKE A DECENT LIVING FROM HERE ON IN? CAN I TAKE CARE OF MYSELF AND MY WIFE AND KID?

IT'S SOMETHING I'LL MAYBE ALWAYS WORRY ABOUT, EVEN IF THE BOOKS I'M SLATED TO DO FOR CURRENT PUBLISHERS SELL REAL WELL.

I'VE ALWAYS DREAMED OF BEING ABLE TO RELAX AND FEEL TROUBLE-FREE FOR LONG STRETCHES OF TIME. I'M 65 NOW. WILL IT EVER HAPPEN?

THE END?

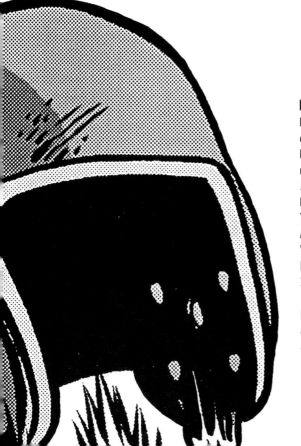

Harvey Pekar was born in 1939 in Cleveland, Ohio which has been his home all his life. After completing high school he went through a series of flunky jobs, tried the Navy and college all to no avail. Finally in 1965 he landed a job with the federal government, which he held until his retirement in 2001. Pekar began his writing career as a jazz critic for *The Jazz Review* in 1959. He began writing comic book stories in 1972, encouraged by his friend Robert Crumb, who has illustrated a number of his pieces. The first collected edition of Pekar's comic AMERICAN SPLENDOR won the American Book Award in 1987. In 1994, the graphic novel OUR CANCER YEAR (on which he collaborated with his wife Joyce Brabner) won the Harvey Award. A movie version of AMERICAN SPLENDOR was released in 2003 and garnered awards at the Sundance and Cannes film festivals.

Native New Yorker **Dean Haspiel** is the creator of BILLY DOGMA and author of super-semi-auto-bio romance comix who occasionally mangles franchise characters. Please visit: www.deanhaspiel.com

THE Quitter

All Photographs courtesy of Harvey Pekar

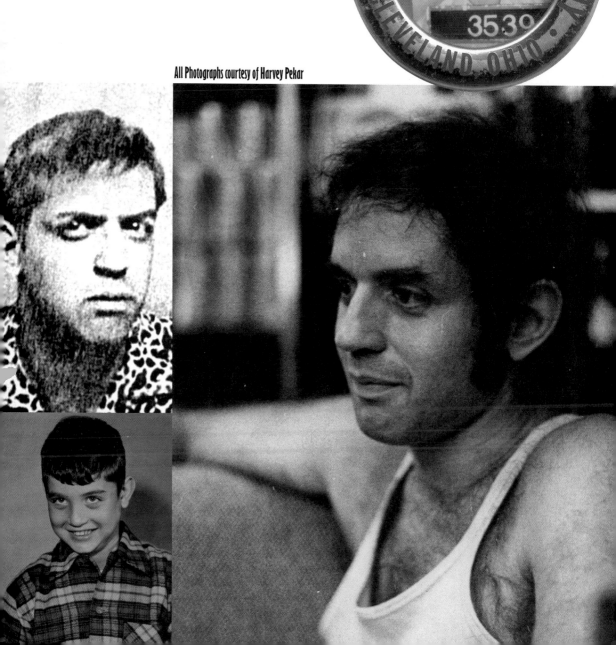

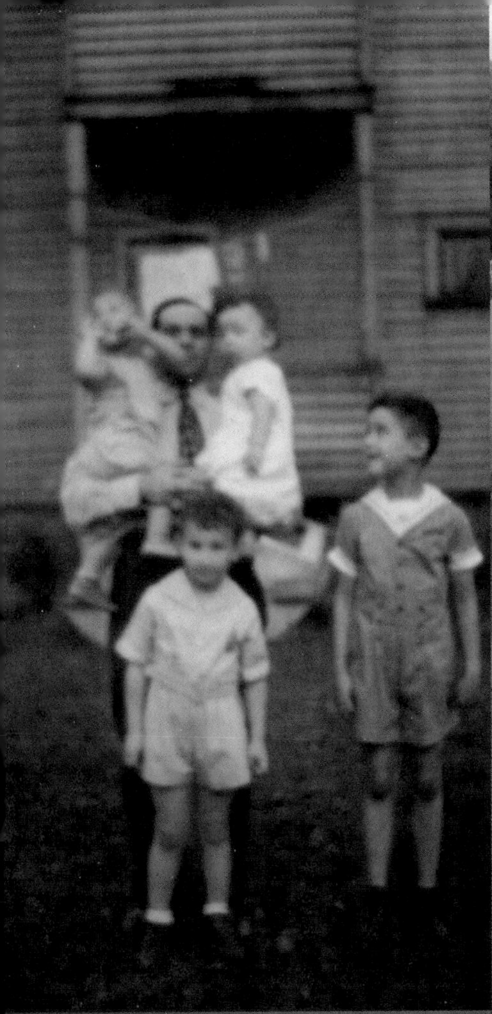

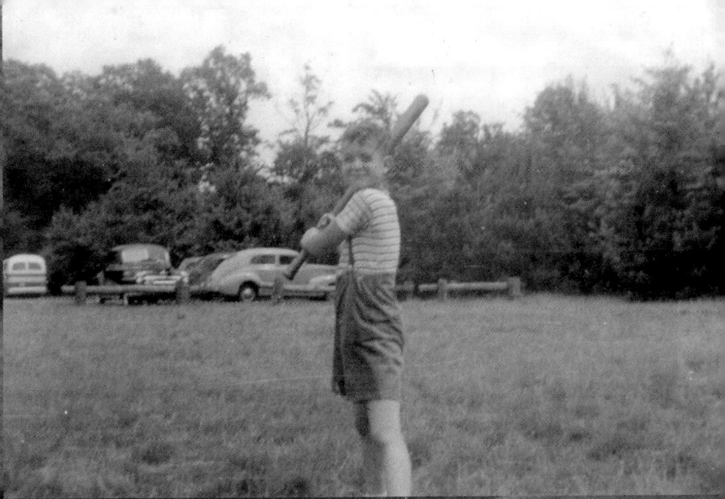

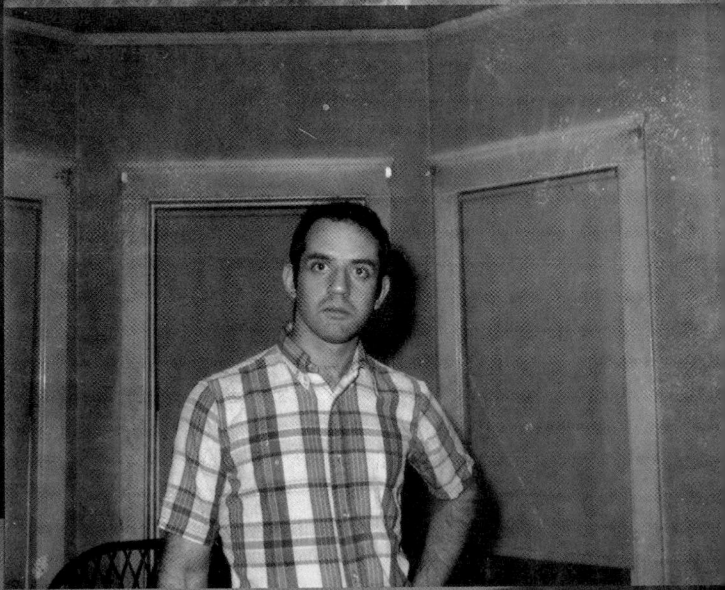

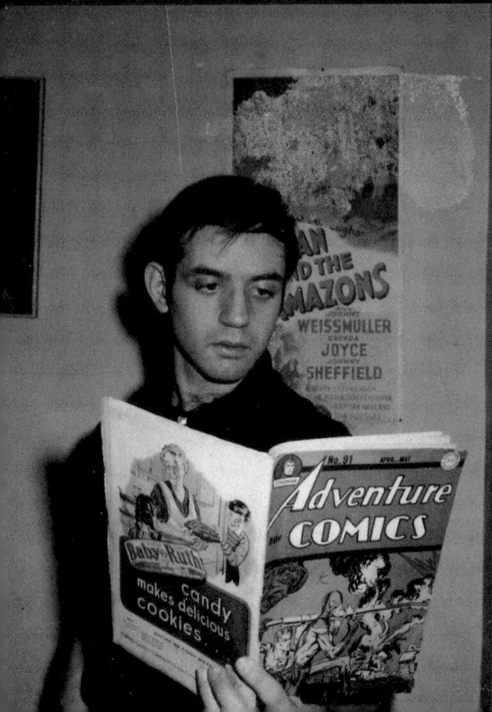
WEISSMULLER
JOYCE
SHEFFIELD
No. 91
Adventure
COMICS
Baby Ruth
candy
makes delicious
cookies.

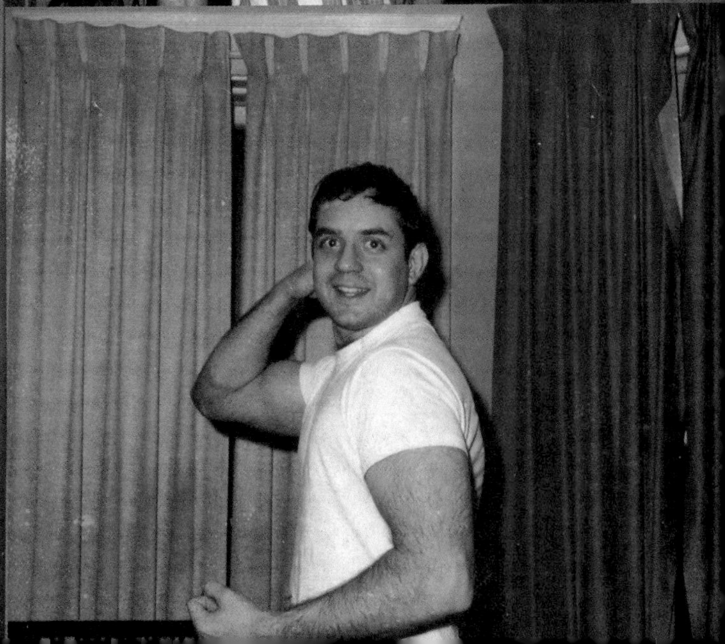

Look for these other VERTIGO books:

100 BULLETS
Brian Azzarello/Eduardo Risso
With one special briefcase, Agent Graves gives you the chance to kill without retribution. But what is the real price for this chance — and who is setting it?
Volume 1: FIRST SHOT, LAST CALL
Volume 2: SPLIT SECOND CHANCE
Volume 3: HANG UP ON THE HANG LOW
Volume 4: A FOREGONE TOMORROW
Volume 5: THE COUNTERFIFTH DETECTIVE
Volume 6: SIX FEET UNDER THE GUN
Volume 7: SAMURAI
Volume 8: THE HARD WAY

ANIMAL MAN
Grant Morrison/Chas Truog/
Doug Hazlewood/various
A minor super-hero's consciousness is raised higher and higher until he becomes aware of his own fictitious nature in this revolutionary and existential series.
Volume 1: ANIMAL MAN
Volume 2: ORIGIN OF THE SPECIES
Volume 3: DEUS EX MACHINA

THE BOOKS OF MAGIC
John Ney Rieber/Peter Gross/various
The continuing trials and adventures of Tim Hunter, whose magical talents bring extra trouble and confusion to his adolescence.
Volume 1: BINDINGS
Volume 2: SUMMONINGS
Volume 3: RECKONINGS
Volume 4: TRANSFORMATIONS
Volume 5: GIRL IN THE BOX
Volume 6: THE BURNING GIRL
Volume 7: DEATH AFTER DEATH

DOOM PATROL
Grant Morrison/Richard Case/
John Nyberg/Doug Braithwaite/various
The World's Strangest Heroes are reimagined even stranger and more otherworldly in this groundbreaking series exploring the mysteries of identity and madness.
Volume 1: CRAWLING FROM THE WRECKAGE
Volume 2: THE PAINTING THAT ATE PARIS

FABLES
Bill Willingham/Lan Medina/
Mark Buckingham/Steve Leialoha
The immortal characters of popular fairy tales have been driven from their homelands and now live hidden among us, trying to cope with life in 21st-century Manhattan.

Volume 1: LEGENDS IN EXILE
Volume 2: ANIMAL FARM
Volume 3: STORYBOOK LOVE
Volume 4: MARCH OF THE WOODEN SOLDIERS
Volume 5: THE MEAN SEASONS

HELLBLAZER
Jamie Delano/Garth Ennis/
Warren Ellis/Brian Azzarello/
Steve Dillon/Marcelo Frusin/various
Where horror, dark magic, and bad luck meet, John Constantine is never far away.
ORIGINAL SINS
DANGEROUS HABITS
FEAR AND LOATHING
TAINTED LOVE
DAMNATION'S FLAME
RAKE AT THE GATES OF HELL
SON OF MAN
HAUNTED
SETTING SUN
HARD TIME
GOOD INTENTIONS
FREEZES OVER
HIGHWATER
RARE CUTS
RED SEPULCHRE
BLACK FLOWERS
CONSTANTINE: THE HELLBLAZER COLLECTION

THE INVISIBLES
Grant Morrison/various
The saga of a terrifying conspiracy and the resistance movement combatting it — a secret underground of ultra-cool guerrilla cells trained in ontological and physical anarchy.
Volume 1: SAY YOU WANT A REVOLUTION
Volume 2: APOCALIPSTICK
Volume 3: ENTROPY IN THE U.K.
Volume 4: BLOODY HELL IN AMERICA
Volume 5: COUNTING TO NONE
Volume 6: KISSING MR. QUIMPER
Volume 7: THE INVISIBLE KINGDOM

LUCIFER
Mike Carey/Peter Gross/Scott Hampton/
Chris Weston/Dean Ormston/various
Walking out of Hell (and out of the pages of THE SANDMAN), an ambitious Lucifer Morningstar creates a new cosmos modelled after his own image.
Volume 1: DEVIL IN THE GATEWAY
Volume 2: CHILDREN AND MONSTERS
Volume 3: A DALLIANCE WITH THE DAMNED

Volume 4: THE DIVINE COMEDY
Volume 5: INFERNO
Volume 6: MANSIONS OF THE SILENCE
Volume 7: EXODUS
Volume 8: THE WOLF BENEATH THE TREE

PREACHER
Garth Ennis/Steve Dillon/various
A modern American epic of life, death, God, love, and redemption — filled with sex, booze, and blood.
Volume 1: GONE TO TEXAS
Volume 2: UNTIL THE END OF THE WORLD
Volume 3: PROUD AMERICANS
Volume 4: ANCIENT HISTORY
Volume 5: DIXIE FRIED
Volume 6: WAR IN THE SUN
Volume 7: SALVATION
Volume 8: ALL HELL'S A-COMING
Volume 9: ALAMO

THE SANDMAN
Neil Gaiman/various
One of the most acclaimed and celebrated comics titles ever published — a rich blend of modern myth and dark fantasy in which contemporary fiction, historical drama, and legend are seamlessly interwoven.
Volume 1: PRELUDES & NOCTURNES
Volume 2: THE DOLL'S HOUSE
Volume 3: DREAM COUNTRY
Volume 4: SEASON OF MISTS
Volume 5: A GAME OF YOU
Volume 6: FABLES & REFLECTIONS
Volume 7: BRIEF LIVES
Volume 8: WORLDS' END
Volume 9: THE KINDLY ONES
Volume 10: THE WAKE
Volume 11: ENDLESS NIGHTS

SANDMAN MYSTERY THEATRE
Matt Wagner/ Steven T. Seagle/
Guy Davis/John Watkiss/R.G. Taylor
The classic Golden Age crimefighter is reimagined in this series of darkly romantic tales from the noir side of pulp.
Volume 1: THE TARANTULA
Volume 2: THE FACE AND THE BRUTE
Volume 3: THE VAMP

SWAMP THING: DARK GENESIS
Len Wein/Berni Wrightson
A gothic nightmare is brought to life with this horrifying yet poignant story of a man transformed into a monster.

SWAMP THING (1984-1987)
Alan Moore/Stephen Bissette/
John Totleben/Rick Veitch/various
The writer and the series that revolutionized comics — a masterpiece of lyrical fantasy.
Volume 1: SAGA OF THE SWAMP THING
Volume 2: LOVE & DEATH
Volume 3: THE CURSE
Volume 4: A MURDER OF CROWS
Volume 5: EARTH TO EARTH
Volume 6: REUNION
Volume 7: REGENESIS

SWAMP THING (2004-2005)
Andy Diggle/Enrique Breccia/
Joshua Dysart/Timothy Green II
Earth's Elemental returns to his roots.
BAD SEED
LOVE IN VAIN

TRANSMETROPOLITAN
Warren Ellis/Darick Robertson/various
An exuberant trip into a frenetic future, where outlaw journalist Spider Jerusalem battles hypocrisy, corruption, and sobriety.
Volume 1: BACK ON THE STREET
Volume 2: LUST FOR LIFE
Volume 3: YEAR OF THE BASTARD
Volume 4: THE NEW SCUM
Volume 5: LONELY CITY
Volume 6: GOUGE AWAY
Volume 7: SPIDER'S THRASH
Volume 8: DIRGE
Volume 9: THE CURE
Volume 10: ONE MORE TIME
Volume 0: TALES OF HUMAN WASTE

Y: THE LAST MAN
Brian K. Vaughan/Pia Guerra/José
Marzán, Jr.
An unexplained plague kills every male mammal on Earth — all except Yorick Brown and his pet monkey. Will he survive this new, emasculated world to discover what killed his fellow men?
Volume 1: UNMANNED
Volume 2: CYCLES
Volume 3: ONE SMALL STEP
Volume 4: SAFEWORD
Volume 5: RING OF TRUTH

100%
Paul Pope

ADVENTURES IN THE RIFLE BRIGADE
Garth Ennis/Carlos Ezquerra

ALL HIS ENGINES
Mike Carey/Leonardo Manco

BARNUM!
Howard Chaykin/David Tischman/
Niko Henrichon

BITE CLUB
Howard Chaykin/
David Tischman/David Hahn

BLOOD: A TALE
J.M. DeMatteis/Kent Williams

THE FILTH
Grant Morrison/Chris Weston/
Gary Erskine

HEAVY LIQUID
Paul Pope

HUMAN TARGET
Peter Milligan/Edvin Biukovic

HUMAN TARGET: FINAL CUT
Peter Milligan/
Javier Pulido

IT'S A BIRD...
Steven T. Seagle/
Teddy Kristiansen

KING DAVID
Kyle Baker

THE ORIGINALS
Dave Gibbons

PROPOSITION PLAYER
Bill Willingham/Paul Guinan/
Ron Randall

UNDERCOVER GENIE
Kyle Baker

V FOR VENDETTA
Alan Moore/David Lloyd

WE3
Grant Morrison/Frank Quitely

THE WITCHING HOUR
Jeph Loeb/Chris Bachalo/
Art Thibert

WHY I HATE SATURN
Kyle Baker

YOU ARE HERE
Kyle Baker